Looking After
Your Computer
for the Older
Generation

Other "Older Generation" Titles

Looking After Your Computer for the Older Generation

Robert Penfold

Bernard Babani (publishing) Ltd
The Grampians
Shepherds Bush Road
London W6 7NF
England
www.babanibooks.com

Please note

Although every care has been taken with the production of this book to ensure that any projects, designs, modifications, and/or programs, etc., contained herewith, operate in a correct and safe manner and also that any components specified are normally available in Great Britain, the Publisher and Author do not accept responsibility in any way for the failure (including fault in design) of any projects, design, modification, or program to work correctly or to cause damage to any equipment that it may be connected to or used in conjunction with, or in respect of any other damage or injury that may be caused, nor do the Publishers accept responsibility in any way for the failure to obtain specified components.

Notice is also given that if any equipment that is still under warranty is modified in any way or used or connected with home-built equipment then that warranty may be void.

© 2004 BERNARD BABANI (publishing) LTD

First Published November 2004

British Library Cataloguing in Publication Data

A catalogue record for this book is available from the British Library

ISBN   0 85934 608 0

Cover Design by Gregor Arthur

Printed and bound in Great Britain by Cox and Wyman

Preface

In an ideal world you would take your new PC system home, plug it all in, switch it on, and everything would work perfectly for the next several years. In the real world the computer is almost certain to work perfectly at first, but there can be a "downhill all the way" element to things thereafter. You tend to get the feeling that your PC is growing old before its time. This gradual tail-off in performance is avoidable though. There are really two aspects to keeping a PC running like new throughout its lifetime.

One is to keep it free from viruses, worms, adware, and all the other unwanted material that tends to flow into your PC via the Internet. PC security is a major issue these days, and it is a topic that has hit the news headlines on a number of occasions in recent years. It is certainly an aspect of computing that can not be ignored by anyone who uses the Internet. Fortunately, some simple and inexpensive measures should be sufficient to keep your PC free from viruses and other computer "pests". The first three chapters of this book cover various security matters, and explain how to keep your PC "clean".

Even if your PC is kept free from viruses and other infections it is likely that there will be a noticeable reduction in performance over a period of time. This is usually the result of what has become termed "computer bloat". With use there is a steady increase in the number of files stored on the computer's hard disc, and the efficiency with which the files are stored tends to decrease. The final chapters of this book cover the safe removal of unwanted files, maintaining optimum hard disc performance, and general information about tuning your PC and keeping it at the peak of efficiency.

Robert Penfold

Trademarks

Contents

1

The basics of security 1

2

Antivirus software 55

3

Spam, spam, spam 109

4

Windows tuning tools 143

5

Uninstalling programs 209

6

Tuning programs 233

7

Backup and Restore 257

The basics
of security

From all sides

Computer security has been a growth industry in
recent years, with ever more ways of protecting PCs
being devised in response to increasingly imaginative
ways of attacking them. Viruses are the best known
form of computer attack, but there are other ways
that hackers can mount an assault on your PC. In
fact many of the much publicised computer viruses
are not, strictly speaking, viruses at all. However, it
is cold comfort to know that your computer problems
are due to a worm and not a virus.

The non-technical press tend to call any form of
software that attacks computers a virus. A virus is a
specific type of program though, and represents just
one of several types that can attack a computer.
Initially, someone attaches the virus to a piece of
software, and then finds a way of getting that software
into computer systems. These days the Internet is
the most likely route for the infection to be spread,
but it is important not to overlook the fact that there
are other means of propagating viruses. Indeed,
computer viruses were being spread around the world
long before the Internet came along.

Programs and possibly other files can carry viruses regardless of the source. If someone gives you a floppy disc, CD-ROM, or DVD containing software it is possible that the contents of the disc are infected with a virus. In the early days of personal computing the main route for viruses to spread was by way of discs containing illegally copied programs. Discs containing pirated software are still used to propagate viruses. Avoid any dodgy software if you wish to keep your PC virus-free.

A later development was pirated software placed on bulletin boards so that it could be downloaded by computer users having PCs equipped with a modem. A modem was an expensive piece of equipment in those days, but once someone had downloaded a piece of software they would usually make several copies and distribute them to friends who would in turn make and distribute further copies. Although the old bulletin board system was crude compared with the modern Internet, it was actually remarkably quick and efficient at spreading viruses.

The main way in which viruses are now spread is much the same as the bulletin board method, but with the Internet acting as the initial source. Due to the popularity of the Internet it is possible for viruses to rapidly spread around the world via this route.

Anyway, having introduced a virus into a system via one route or another, it will attack that system and try to replicate itself. Some viruses only attack the boot sector of a system disc. This is the part of the disc that the computer uses to boot into the operating system. Other viruses will try to attach themselves to any file of the appropriate type, which usually means a program file of some sort. The attraction of a program file is that the user will probably run the program before too long, which gives the virus a chance to spread the infection and (or) start attacking the computer system.

At one time there were only two possible ways in which a virus could attack a computer. One way was for the virus to attach itself to a program file that the user then ran on his or her computer. The other was for someone to leave an infected floppy disc in the computer when it was switched off. On switching the computer on again the floppy disc was used as the boot disc, activating the virus in the disc's boot sector.

Script virus

These days you have to be suspicious of many more types of file. Many applications programs such as word processors and spreadsheets have the ability to automate tasks using scripts or macros as they are also known. The application effectively has a built-in programming language and the script or macro is a form of program. This makes it possible for viruses or other harmful programs to be present in many types of data file. Scripts are also used in some web pages, and viruses can be hidden in these JavaScript programs, Java applets, etc. There are other potential sources of infection such as Email attachments.

I would not wish to give the impression that all files, web pages, and Emails are potential sources of script or macro viruses. There are some types of file where there is no obvious way for them to carry a virus or other harmful program. A simple text file for example, should be completely harmless. Even in cases where a harmful program is disguised as a text file with a "txt" extension, the file should be harmless. The system will treat it as a text file and it can not be run provided no one alters the file extension. Similarly, an Email that contains a plain text message can not contain a script virus. Nevertheless, it is probably best to regard all files and Emails with a degree of suspicion.

Benign virus

It tends to be assumed that all viruses try to harm the infected computer system. This is not correct though, and many viruses actually do very little. For example, you might find that nothing more occurs than a daft message appears onscreen when a certain date is reached, or on a particular date each year. Viruses such as this certainly have a degree of nuisance value, but they are not harmful. I would not wish to give the impression that most viruses are harmless. Many computer viruses do indeed try to do serious damage to the infected system. If in doubt you have to assume that a virus is harmful.

A virus that does attack the system will often go for the boot sector of the hard disc drive, and this will usually make it impossible to boot the computer into the operating system. Other viruses attack the FAT (file allocation table) in an attempt to effectively scramble the contents of the disc. The data is left intact by this type of attack, but without a valid FAT there is no way of knowing what files are on the disc, or which bits of the disc make up each file. Consequently, your chances of recovering the data are slim. Another way of attacking the files on the disc is to take the direct approach and simply alter all or part of their contents. Renaming or simply deleting files are other popular ploys.

Worm

A worm is a program that replicates itself, usually from one disc to another, or from one system to another via a local area network (LAN) or the Internet. Like a virus, a worm is not necessarily harmful. In recent times many of the worldwide virus scares have actually been caused by worms transmitted via Email, and not by what would normally be accepted as a virus. The usual ploy is for the worm to send a copy of itself to every address in the Email address book of the infected system.

A worm spread in this way, even if it is not intrinsically harmful, can have serious consequences. There can be a sudden upsurge in the amount of Email traffic, possibly causing parts of the Email system to seriously slow down or even crash. Some worms compromise the security of the infected system, perhaps enabling it to be used by a hacker for sending spam for example.

Trojan horse

A Trojan horse, or just plain Trojan as it is now often called, is a program that is supposed to be one thing but is actually another. In the early days many Trojans were in the form of free software, and in particular, free antivirus programs. The users obtained nasty shocks when the programs were run, with their computer systems being attacked. Like viruses, some Trojans do nothing more than display stupid messages, but others attack the disc files, damage the boot sector of the hard disc, and so on.

Backdoor Trojan

A backdoor Trojan is the same as the standard variety in that it is supplied in the form of a program that is supposed to be one thing but is actually another. In some cases nothing appears to happen when you install the program. In other cases the program might actually install and run as expected. In both cases one or two small programs will have been installed on the computer and set to run when the computer is booted.

One ploy is to have programs that produce log files showing which programs you have run and Internet sites that you have visited. The log will usually include any key presses as well. The idea is for the log file to provide passwords to things such as your Email account, online bank account, and so on. Someone hacking into your computer system will usually look for the log files, and could obviously gain access to important information from these files.

Another ploy is to have a program that makes it easier for hackers to break into your computer system. A backdoor Trojan does not attack the infected computer in the same way as some viruses, and it does not try to spread the infection to other discs or computers. Potentially though, a backdoor Trojan is more serious than a virus, particularly if you use the computer for online banking, share dealing, etc.

Spyware

Spyware programs monitor system activity and send information to another computer by way of the Internet. There are really two types of spyware, and one tries to obtain passwords and send them to another computer. This takes things a step further than the backdoor Trojan programs mentioned earlier. A backdoor Trojan makes it easier for a hacker to obtain sensitive information from your PC, but it does not go as far as sending any information that is placed in the log files. Spyware is usually hidden in other software in Trojan fashion.

Adware

The second type of spyware is more correctly called adware. In common with spyware, it gathers information and sends it to another computer via the

Internet. Adware is not designed to steal passwords or other security information from your PC. Its purpose is usually to gather information for marketing purposes, and this typically means gathering and sending details of the web sites you have visited. Some free programs are supported by banner advertising, and the adware is used to select advertisements that are likely to be of interest to you.

Programs that are supported by adware have not always made this fact clear during the installation process. Sometimes the use of adware was pointed out in the End User License Agreement, but probably few people bother to read the "fine print". These days the more respectable software companies that use this method of raising advertising revenues make it clear that the adware will be installed together with the main program. There is often the option of buying a "clean" copy of the program. Others try to con you into installing the adware by using the normal tricks.

Provided you know that it is being installed and are happy to have it on your PC, adware is not a major security risk. It is sending information about your surfing habits, but you have given permission for it to do so. If you feel that this is an invasion of privacy, then do not consent to it being installed. The situation is different if you are tricked into installing adware. Then it does clearly become an invasion of your privacy and you should remove any software of this type from your PC. Note that if you consent to adware being installed on your PC and then change your mind, removing it will probably result in the free software it supports being disabled or uninstalled.

Dialers

A dialer is a program that uses a modem and an ordinary dial-up connection to connect your PC to another computer system. Dialers probably have numerous legitimate applications, but they are mainly associated with various types of scam. An early one was a promise of free pornographic material that required a special program to be downloaded. This program was, of course, the dialer, which proceeded to call a high cost number in a country thousands of miles away. In due course the user received an astronomic telephone bill.

A modern variation on this is where users are tricked into downloading a dialer, often with the promise of free software of some description. Users go onto the Internet in the usual way via their dial-up connections, and everything might appear to be perfectly normal. What is actually happening though is that they are not connecting to the Internet via their normal Internet service provider (ISP). Instead, the dialer is connecting them to a different ISP that is probably thousands of miles away and is costing a fortune in telephone charges. Again, the problem is very apparent when the telephone bill arrives.

The increasing use of broadband Internet connections has largely or totally removed the threat of dialer-related problems for many. If there is no ordinary telephone modem in your PC, there is no way the dialer can connect your PC to the Internet or another computer system via a dial-up connection. There is a slight risk if your PC is equipped with a telephone modem for sending and receiving faxes. The risk is relatively small though, since you would presumably notice that the modem was being used for no apparent reason.

Anyway, if your PC has an ordinary modem that is connected to a telephone socket, you have to be on your guard against dialers. This problem has received much publicity recently, with many computer users being duped and receiving large telephone bills. It is not just a few unlucky users that have been caught out by these scams.

Hoax virus

A hoax virus might sound innocuous enough and just a bit of a joke, but it has the potential to spread across the world causing damage to computer systems. The hoax is usually received in the form of an Email from someone that has contacted you previously. They say that the Email they sent you previously was infected with a virus, and the Email then goes on to provide information on how to remove the virus. This usually entails searching for one or more files on your PC's hard disc drive and erasing them.

Of course, there was no virus in the initial Email. The person that sent the initial Email could be the hoaxer, or they might have been fooled by the hoax themselves. The hoax Email suggests that you contact everyone that you have emailed recently, telling them that their computer could be infected and giving them the instructions for the "cure". This is the main way in which a hoax virus is propagated. The files that you are instructed to remove could be of no real consequence, or they could be important system files. It is best not to fall for the hoax and find out which.

These hoax viruses demonstrate the point that all the antivirus software in the world will not provide full protection for your PC. They are simple text files that do not do any direct harm to your PC, and can not be kept at bay by software. Ultimately it is up to you to use some common sense and provide the final line of defence. A quick check on the Internet will usually provide details of hoax viruses and prevent you from doing anything silly.

Note that there are other scams that involve hoax emails. Recently there have been several instances of Emails being sent to customers of online financial companies. These purport to come from the company concerned, and they ask customers to provide their passwords and other account details. A link is provided to the site, and the site usually looks quite convincing. It is not the real thing though, and anyone falling for it has their account details stolen. The success of this scan has been limited, but some accounts have been plundered. This method of tricking people into providing passwords, etc., is called "phishing".

Basic measures

The obvious way of protecting a PC from viruses and other harmful programs is to simply keep it away from possible sources of infection. Unfortunately, the quarantine approach is not usually a practical one. If you use a PC to (say) produce letters that are printed out and then sent by post, then the quarantine method should work. Once the computer has been set up ready for use it should not be necessary to put any discs into the floppy or CD-ROM drives, and there is no need for it to connect to the Internet or any other network. It might be necessary to have a CD/RW disc or two for backup purposes, but provided these discs are not used in any other computer there is no significant risk of them introducing a virus into the computer.

Unfortunately, little real world computing is compatible with this standalone approach. I use my PC to produce letters that are sent through the post, but I probably send about 50 times as many Emails. Large numbers of Emails are also received in my Email accounts. My PC is used mainly for generating work that is sent off on CDR discs, but I also receive data discs occasionally, and these have to be read using my computer. I have to use the Internet extensively for research, and I sometimes download software updates. Isolating my computer from the outside world would render it largely useless to me. These days most computer users are in a similar position.

Totally removing the threat of attack is not usually possible, but the chances of a successful attack can be greatly reduced by using a few basic precautions.

Email attachments

Some individuals operate a policy of never opening Email attachments. I do not take things that far, but I would certainly not open an Email attachment unless I new the sender of the Email and was expecting the attachment. Bear in mind that some viruses and worms spread by hijacking a user's Email address book and sending copies of the infected Email to every address in the address book. The fact that an Email comes from someone you know, or purports to, does not guarantee that it is free from infection. Another point to bear in mind is that Email attachments are now the most common way of spreading viruses and computer worms.

Selective downloading

Downloading software updates from the main computer software companies should be safe, as should downloading the popular freebies from their official sources. Downloading just about anything else involves a degree of risk and should be kept to a minimum.

Pirated software

Pirated software has become a major problem for the software companies in recent years. In addition to casual software piracy where friends swap copies of programs there is now an epidemic of commercial copying. Apart from the fact that it is illegal to buy and use pirate software, some of it contains viruses, spyware, etc.

Virus protection

Some programs, and particularly those from Microsoft, have built-in virus protection that is designed to block known macro/script viruses. If you have any programs that include this feature, make sure that it is enabled.

P2P

P2P (peer to peer) programs are widely used for file swapping. Even if you use this type of software for swapping legal (non-pirated) files, it still has to be regarded as very risky. In most cases you have no idea who is supplying the files, or whether they are what they are supposed to be. Also, you are providing others with access to your PC, and this access could be exploited by hackers.

Switch off

Some PC users leave their computers running continuously in the belief that it gives better reliability. It did in the days when computers were based on valves, but there is no evidence that it improves reliability with modern computers. It will increase your electricity bills, and it also increases the vulnerability of your PC if it has some form of always-on Internet connection. No one can hack into your computer system if it is switched off.

Prevention

The old adage about "prevention is better than cure" certainly applies to computer viruses. In addition to some basic security precautions, equip your PC with antivirus software and keep it up-to-date. This software will usually detect and deal with viruses before they have a chance to spread the infection or do any damage to your files.

Backup

Always have a least one backup copy of any important data file. This is not just a matter of having a replacement copy if a file should be destroyed by a virus. The hard disc of a computer has a finite lifespan, and hard disc failures are not a rarity. You should backup all important data anyway, just in case there is a major hard disc failure. It is a good idea to backup the entire system from time to time. This makes it easy to restore a working version of the system, applications programs, etc., in the event of any major problem such as a virus attack, corrupted Windows installation, or hard disc failure.

Up-to-date

Many viruses and worms are designed to exploit a security flaw in an applications program or the operating system itself. Sometimes these flaws have already been covered by software updates, but not everyone has bothered to update their PCs and the infection is able to spread. In fairness to amateur PC users, there have been worms that have exploited old

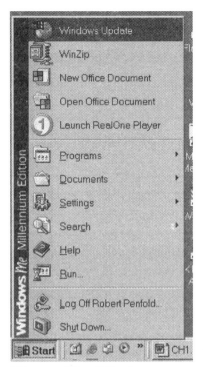

Fig.1.1 The Windows Update option

security "holes" in the operating systems of servers. The professionals maintaining the affected servers had not bothered to routinely update their systems. Some worms and viruses exploit previously unknown security flaws, but patches to fix the problem are soon made available when this sort of thing occurs.

Some applications programs now have an automatic update facility, as does the Windows operating system. A system such as this could be regarded as a potential security risk itself, but manual updates are usually available from the software publisher's web site if you do not trust the automatic approach. In the case of Windows it is possible to launch the automatic update facility via the Windows Update option in the start menu (Figure 1.1). The computer used in this example is running Windows ME, but the process is exactly the same for Windows XP users. Of course, the PC must have an active Internet

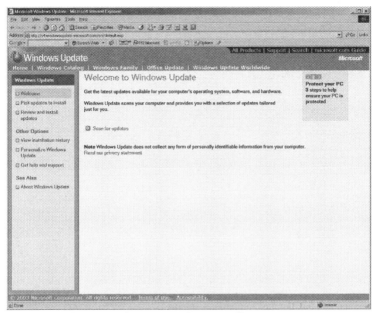

Fig.1.2 The Windows Update Welcome screen

connection in order to use any form of online update system.

The Windows update system produces the Welcome screen of Figure 1.2, and the first step is to operate the Scan for Updates link near the middle of the page. The scanning process is usually quite quick and produces a list of available updates in the left-hand section of the screen (Figure 1.3). Left-clicking an entry brings up a list of available updates in that category. The list, together with details of each update, is displayed in the main section of the window, as in Figure 1.4. In this example only one update is listed, but this is a security type that needs to be installed. It is as well to look through the other

1 The basics of security

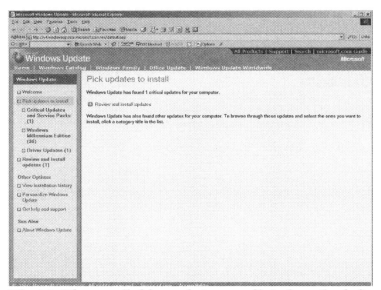

Fig.1.3 The available updates are listed on the left

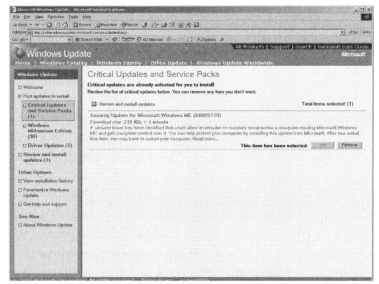

Fig.1.4 Selecting a category provides more details

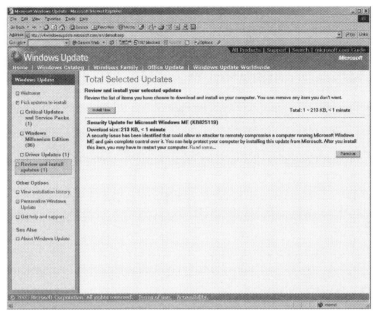

Fig.1.5   Operate the Install button to go ahead with the updates

categories to see if there is anything worth installing, but you will probably find that many of the updates are not of relevance to the Windows installation you are using. There might be foreign language updates for example.

Having selected the required updates via the Add and Remove buttons, activate the Review and Install Updates link in the left-hand section of the window. Then operate the Install button in the main section of the window (Figure 1.5). The updates will then be installed and a small window will show how the process is progressing (Figure 1.6). Once the updates have been installed you will be asked if you would like

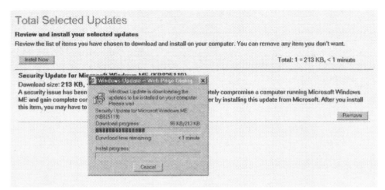

Fig.1.6   The small window shows how things are progressing

to reboot the computer. It is not essential to do so, but the updates will not take effect until the computer has been rebooted.

Browser configuration

The Internet Explorer browser program has some built-in safeguards to help protect your computer from an attack via the Internet. It is possible to vary the degree of protection provided by the browser, which might seem to be an odd way of doing things. Surely it would be safer to have the browser automatically set for the highest possible degree of security? Clearly it would, but the total security approach to things would also mean that many useful features would fail to work. For example, with the maximum level of security it is not possible to download any files, which is a major limitation. You probably use web sites that require users to log on, but most of these sites have a facility that

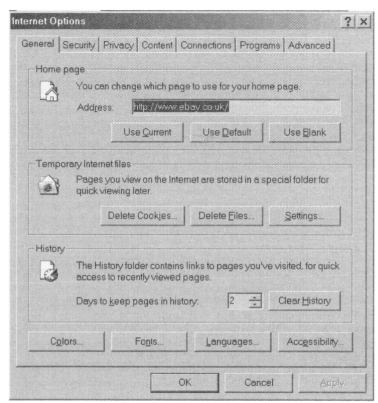

Fig.1.7 The Internet Options window

automatically logs users onto the system. Facilities of this type will not work if a browser is set for maximum security.

The easy way of altering the security setting of Internet Explorer is to run the program and then select Internet Options from the Tools menu. This produces a window like the one of Figure 1.7, and by default the General tab will be selected. The General

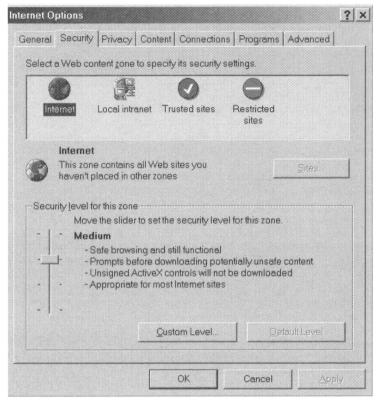

Fig.1.8 The Security options

section is used for altering the homepage and other basic tasks, but it is the Security page that is of interest in the current context.

Selecting the Security tab produces a window like the one in Figure 1.8. The degree of security is selected by way of the slider control, which has four settings. These settings are Low, Medium-Low, Medium, and High. The text next to the slider control gives brief details of each setting, but in practice it is really a

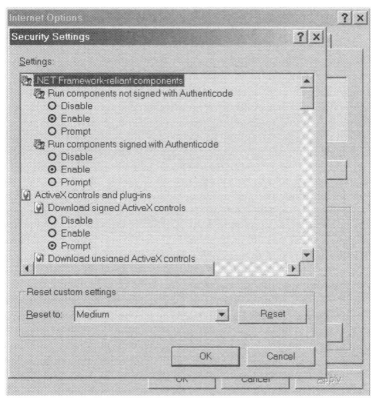

Fig.1.9 More precise control is available

matter of using the "suck it and see" method. Use
the highest level of security that does not result in
any features you use being disabled.

Cookies

More precise control over the security settings can
be obtained by operating the Custom Level button.
A new window (Figure 1.9) is then launched, and this
has radio buttons that are used to individually control

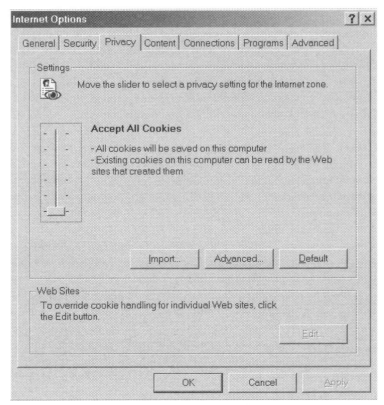

Fig.1.10 The Internet Options Privacy page

each aspect of security. In order to use the custom settings properly it is necessary to understand the terminology involved. One of these terms is "cookies", and with older versions of Windows these are controlled via the Custom Level feature. In Windows ME and XP they are controlled separately by way of the Privacy page, and operating this tab switches the window to look like Figure 1.10.

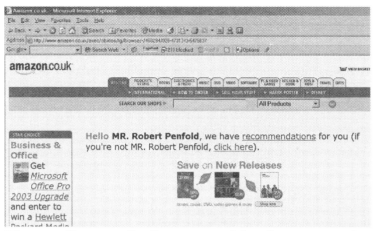

Fig.1.11 Some web sites use cookies for automatic identification

A cookie is just a text file that is deposited on the hard disc drive of your PC when certain web sites are visited. In most cases the use of cookies is optional, but without them you will find that certain features of the site do not work properly. With a few sites you can only use its facilities if your PC is set to accept cookies. Since a cookie is just a small text file it should be completely innocuous. There is a special folder on the hard disc drive for cookies (usually C:\Windows\Cookies), and if you take a look at its contents there will usually be a large number of files there. On my PC I found over 1800 cookies in this directory!

The main use of cookies is to enable a site to automatically identify you on each visit. When I visit www.amazon.co.uk for example, I am greeted with the message "Hello MR. Robert Penfold" (Figure 1.11).

The site identifies me by looking for a cookie left on the hard disc during a previous visit to the site. The site will not know who I am if that cookie is deleted or I use a different PC to access the site. Indeed, if I use a PC belonging to someone else and that person has used the Amazon site, it is the greeting for that person that I will receive.

This is a slight drawback of cookies. Anyone gaining access to your PC can take advantage of the cookies it contains. In practice cookies do not give automatic access to anything important. The site of your Email provider might recognise you via a cookie, but you still have to use a password in order to gain access to your Email account. Consequently, someone gaining access to your computer and the cookies it contains should not permit them to access any important accounts. However, never leave passwords anywhere on your PC. Storing passwords on a PC is a bit like locking a door but going off and leaving the key in the lock.

In some cases cookies will provide automatic entry to subscription or other password-protected sites. Bear in mind that anyone gaining access to your PC will also gain access to these sites if you opt for the convenience of automatic entry. Furthermore, they will gain access to the sites via your account and in your name. Fortunately, it is unlikely that they will be able to do any real harm since things such as online bank accounts require users to login properly at each visit. Do not opt for automatic entry to any site that contains personal information.

One slight problem with cookies is that they tend to build up on your hard disc drive, especially if you use the Internet for research and visit many sites per day. I think that the importance of this tends to be exaggerated somewhat, since the files are small and will each consume whatever the minimum amount per file happens to be for your PC. Eventually some 25 to 50 megabytes could be used, but with most hard discs having a capacity of 20,000 megabytes or more this is rather less important than in the days of 500 megabyte discs.

The "belt and braces" approach to removing unwanted cookies is to simply remove all cookies from your PC. This will clearly remove the useful ones along with the rubbish, but the useful ones will be restored on signing in to your favourite web sites again. In order to remove all cookies it is just a matter of launching Internet Explorer, selecting Internet Options from the Tools menu, and then operating the Delete Cookies button in the middle section of the window. Operate the Yes button when asked if you are sure that you wish to delete the cookies.

Many PCs are supplied complete with a suite of utility programs, or you might have bought and installed one. Many of these suites include a utility that helps to identify cookies so that you can remove any that are for sites that are no longer of any interest. There are also shareware utilities that provide this function, and these can be downloaded and tried for free. You only pay for the program if you intend to go on using it. Many cookie related programs can be found at www.shareware.com and similar sites.

In addition to programs that enable unwanted cookies to be deleted there are programs that delete a cookie once the current session has been ended. Some cookies are automatically deleted anyway, and these are known as "session-only" or "per-session" cookies. These programs effectively turn any desired cookie into a session-only type. If you visit a site where cookies are mandatory, a program that has this facility provides an easy way of removing the cookies once you have exited the site.

Cookie options

The cookie control in the Internet Options window has six settings from Accept All Cookies to Block All Cookies. The text to the right of the control briefly explains the effect of each setting. As cookies are relatively harmless, there is probably no significant danger in using Accept All Cookies setting. Cookies do provide a means for your browsing habits to be monitored, so you may prefer to use a higher setting on privacy rather than security grounds. Bear in mind though, that with the higher settings you will almost certainly find that some of the facilities at your favourite sites fail to work, and all or part of a few sites might be inaccessible.

It is possible to override automatic handling of cookies by operating the Advanced button in the Privacy section of the Internet Options window. This produces

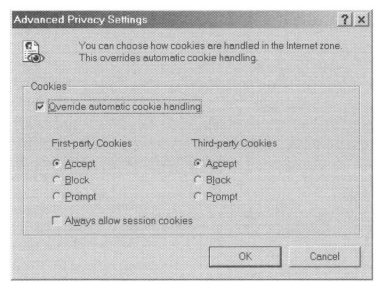

Fig.1.12 The Advanced Privacy Settings window

a window like the one shown in Figure 1.12, and the checkbox near the top must be ticked in order to make the other options active. First and third-party cookies can be blocked, allowed to pass, or you can be prompted each time a site tries to use a cookie. There is a lot to be said for the prompting method, which ensures that only cookies you agree to use find their way onto the hard disc. In practice it might mean a lot of hassle though. Per-session cookies will always be allowed if the checkbox near the bottom of the window is ticked. There is probably nothing to be gained by blocking this type of cookie so it makes sense to tick this checkbox.

Firewalls

A considerable amount of protection can be provided by using the most secure browser settings, but only at the expense of some facilities becoming difficult or impossible to use. There is an alternative in the form of a firewall, which can be either a piece of hardware or a program. A firewall's basic function is much the same whether it is implemented in software or hardware.

Although some people seem to think that a firewall and antivirus programs are the same, there are major differences. There is often some overlap between real world antivirus and firewall programs, but their primary aims are different. An antivirus program is designed to scan files on discs and the contents of the computer's memory in search of viruses and other potentially harmful files. Having found any suspect files, the program will usually deal with them. A firewall is used to block access to your PC, and in most cases it is access to your PC via the Internet that is blocked. However, if you have two or more PCs in a local area network (LAN), a software firewall will usually block access via the network unless it is told to do otherwise.

Of course, a firewall is of no practical value if it blocks communication from one PC to another and access via the Internet. What it is actually doing is preventing unauthorised access to the protected PC. When you access an Internet site your PC sends messages to the server hosting that site, and these messages request the pages you wish to view. Having requested information, the PC expects information to be sent from the appropriate server, and it accepts that information when it is received. A firewall does not interfere with this type of Internet activity provided it is set up correctly.

It is a different matter when another system tries to access your PC when you have not instigated the initial contact. The firewall will treat this attempted entry as an attack and will block it. Of course, the attempt at accessing your PC might not be an attack, and a firewall can result in legitimate access being blocked. Something like P2P file swapping is likely to fail or operate in a limited fashion. The sharing of files and resources on a local area network could also be blocked. A practical firewall enables the user to permit certain types of access so that the computer can work normally while most unauthorised access is still blocked. However, doing so does reduce the degree of protection provided by the firewall.

A firewall should also provide protection against backdoor Trojans, dialers, and other programs that try to send information from your PC via the Internet. When installing a firewall the user gives permission for certain programs to access the Internet. Permission is only granted for programs that will need to access the Internet legitimately, such as web browsers and download managers. An alert will be provided if an unauthorised program such as a dialer tries to access the Internet, with access being automatically blocked. There can be occasional false alarms, with something like an application program trying to use an automatic update facility for example. The user has the option of overriding the firewall and permitting access in such cases.

A firewall used to be considered essential for broadband users, but less important for those having an ordinary dialup Internet connection. Recent problems with dialers, backdoor Trojans, and the like have made it necessary to reassess this situation. A software firewall will prevent dialers and backdoor Trojans from accessing the Internet, and it therefore provides a very worthwhile boost to the security of the protected PC.

Some types of broadband Internet access come complete with a built-in hardware firewall, but it can still be advantageous to have a software firewall. The hardware firewalls built into some types of broadband firewall are excellent at stopping attacks via the Internet. They are usually ineffective at dealing with threats from within the system, such as those from dialers and backdoor Trojans. Hardware firewalls often treat all Internet traffic as legitimate provided it originates from within the PC. In other words, hackers trying to access your PC via the Internet will be blocked, but a backdoor Trojan sending information gathered from your PC will be allowed to go ahead. A software firewall detects and blocks unauthorised Internet accesses that originate in the PC.

Ports

When dealing with firewalls you are almost certain to encounter the term "ports". In a computer context this normally means a socket on the PC where a peripheral of some kind is connected. In an Internet context a port is not in the form of any hardware, and it is more of a software concept. Programs communicate over the Internet via these notional ports that are numbered from 0 to 65535. It enables several programs to utilise the Internet without the data for one program getting directed to another program.

Firewalls usually have the ability to block activity on certain ports. The idea is to block ports that are likely to be used by programs such as backdoor Trojans but are not normally used for legitimate Internet traffic. A Trojan could be set to "listen" on (say) port 80, and send the data it has collected once it receives a message from a hacker. By blocking any activity on port 80, the firewall ensures that the Trojan can not send any data, and that it will not be contacted in the first place.

Note that most software firewall programs will block this type of activity anyway, because the firewall will detect that an unauthorised program is trying to use the Internet. It will alert the user and only permit the data to be sent if the user authorises it. Presumably the user would "smell a rat" and deny permission for the Trojan to access the Internet. Most hardware firewalls would prevent the message from the hacker from reaching the Trojan, and would also prevent the attack from succeeding. Even so, it is useful to block ports that are likely to be used for hacking the system. Doing so makes it that much harder for someone to "crack" your system, which is what Internet security is all about.

False alarms

Many of the early firewall programs had a major problem in that they were a bit overzealous. While you were trying the surf the Internet there were constant interruptions from the firewall informing you of attacks on the system. In reality these attacks were wholly or largely nonexistent. What the programs were actually detecting was normal Internet activity, and many of the false alarms could be prevented by setting up the program to ignore certain programs accessing the Internet. Some of these programs were virtually unusable though.

Modern firewall programs mostly operate in a rather less "in your face" fashion, and produce fewer interruptions. Even so, it is usually necessary to go through a setting up process in order to keep down the number of false alarms, and further tweaking may be needed in order to get things working really well. Of course, if you would like to be informed about every possible attack on the system, most firewalls will duly oblige provided the appropriate settings are used. This certainly gives the ultimate in security, but it could make surfing the Internet a very slow and tedious process.

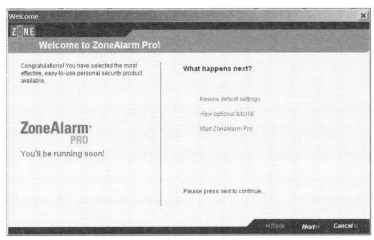

Fig.1.13 The initial screen of Zone Alarm Pro

Zone Alarm

There are plenty of software firewalls to choose from, and most of them are capable of providing your PC with a high degree of security. Fortunately, there are several good firewall programs that cost little or nothing. Zone Alarm is a popular firewall, and it exists in free, trial, and full commercial versions. It is quite easy to set up and use, and the free version represents a good starting point for private users wishing to try a good quality firewall at minimum cost. All versions of this program are quite easy to set up. Zone alarm Pro will be used for this example, and this program has a few more facilities than the basic (free) version.

Figure 1.13 shows the initial window produced once the installation process has been completed. This simply explains that there are a few processes to complete before the program is ready for use. At the

1 The basics of security

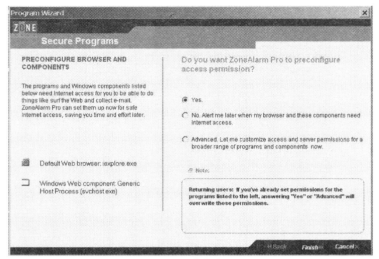

*Fig.1.14 You can choose which programs are
granted Internet access now or later*

next screen (Figure 1.14) Zone Alarm lists programs
that it thinks will need Internet access. The list will

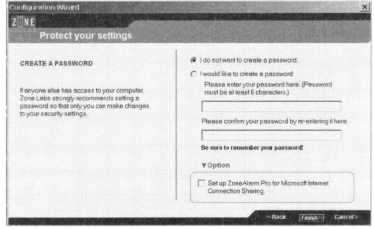

Fig.1.15 Password protection is available

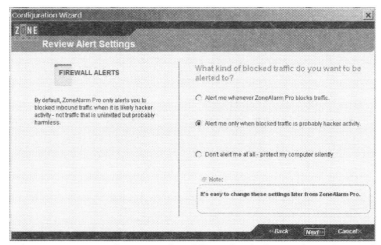

Fig.1.16 Here the required level of alerts is selected

include the default browser and any other programs that are required for normal Internet access. By default, these programs will be given Internet access, but other programs will produce a warning message if they attempt to use the Internet. Access will then be allowed only if you give permission. You might prefer to choose which programs will be granted access during the setting-up process rather than dealing with it later as programs try to access the Internet. As most programs do not require Internet access, it is probably easier to grant access as and when necessary.

The next window (Figure 1.15) enables the program to be password protected. This is only necessary if someone else has access to your PC. Things then move on to a window (Figure 1.16) where you choose

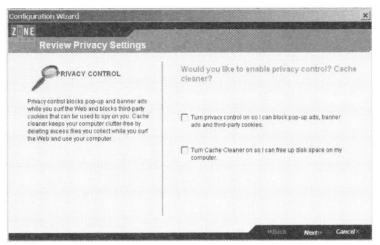

Fig.1.17 Two optional extras are available

the types of Internet access that will produce alerts. You can opt to have an onscreen message appear when any access is blocked, or for no alerts to be issued. Note that the program will still continue to block Internet access as and when it sees fit, even if the alerts are completely switched off. The middle option results in an alert being produced when the program considers that attempted access is probably the result of an attack by a hacker. This is the default option and is probably the best choice.

The options available at the next screen (Figure 1.17) are for two of Zone Alarm Pro's optional extras. One of these is a routine that blocks pop-up advertisements and it also blocks third-party "spy" cookies. Pop-ups are now so widespread on the Internet that they have become a major nuisance.

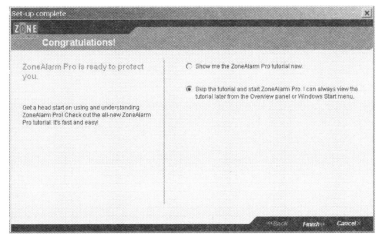

Fig.1.18 You can start the program or view a tutorial

Apart from being irksome, they can effectively slow down your Internet connection by increasing the amount of data that has to be downloaded. This can be a serious drag on your surfing if you do not have some form of broadband connection. A pop-up blocker is therefore a very useful feature.

Cache cleaning is the other option. Copies of many Internet files are kept on a PC so that they do not have to be downloaded again when the relevant pages are revisited. Anyone undertaking a lot of surfing is likely to end up with many megabytes of cached Internet files on their PC's hard disc. These files should eventually be removed by Windows, but the cache cleaner provides a neater solution by preventing a massive build-up from occurring in the first place.

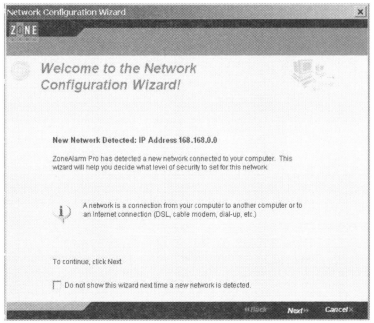

Fig.1.19 A network has been detected

The next window (Figure 1.18) gives the option of starting the program or viewing a quick tutorial. It is definitely a good idea to look at the tutorial, but it can be viewed at any time by running Zone Alarm Pro and operating the Tutorial button.

Network

The PC used for this demonstration has its Internet connection provided by a broadband modem that has a built-in router, with two other PCs connected to the router. This network was detected by Zone Alarm Pro (Figure 1.19), and the Network Configuration

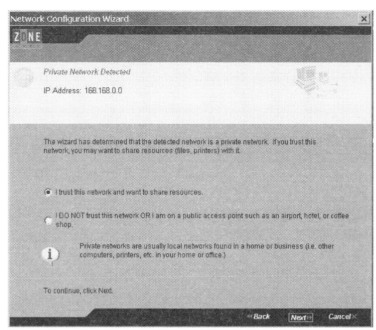

Fig.1.20   The network can be enabled or blocked

Wizard was launched. Remember that a firewall will block any network access, including the LAN (local area network) variety, unless instructed otherwise. At the next screen (Figure 1.20) you have the option of enabling this network or blocking it. Obviously it must be enabled in order to permit the system to go on working properly.

The window of Figure 1.21 enables the network to be given a name of your choice, or you can simply settle for the default name. The next window (Figure 1.22) simply shows the settings you have chosen and provides an opportunity to go back and change them.

1 The basics of security

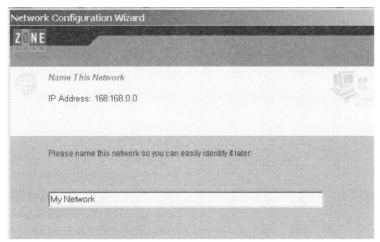

Fig.1.21 A name is provided for the network, or the default can be used

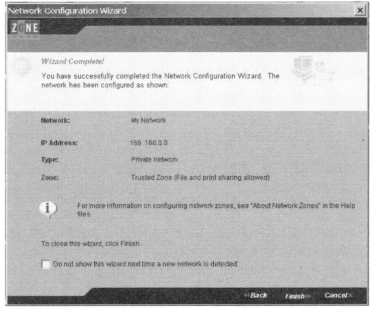

Fig.1.22 The selected settings are listed here

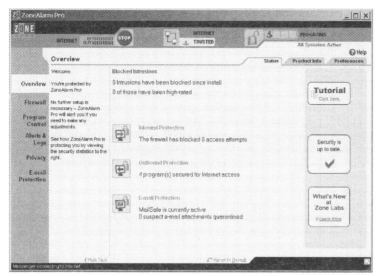

Fig.1.23 Finally, the program is operational

Finally, the program is run (Figure 1.23). In normal use the program runs in the background and it is only necessary to go to this screen if you need to make changes to the setup or view the statistics produced by the program.

Operating the Firewall tab switches the window to look like Figure 1.24, and the degree of security in each zone can then be adjusted via the slider controls. Unless there is good reason to change the setting for the Internet Zone, it should be left at High. The other tabs permit easy control of other aspects of the program, such as alerts (Figure 1.25). Therefore, if you find any of the initial settings unsatisfactory it is easy to change them.

1 The basics of security

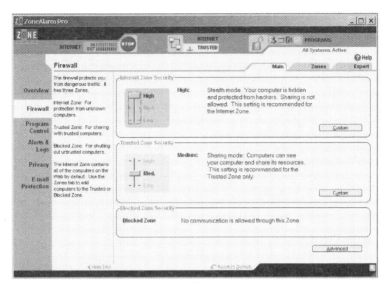

Fig.1.24 Here the Firewall tab has been operated

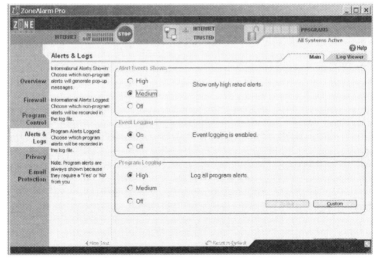

Fig.1.25 The settings can be changed when this tab is selected

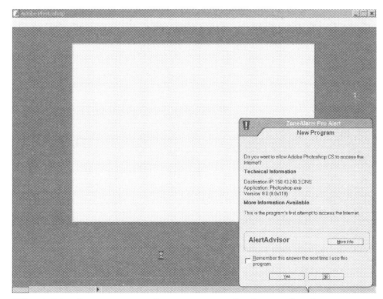

Fig.1.26 A program has generated an alert

In use it is likely that the program will initially query potential problems that are really just a normal part of the PC's operation. In the example of Figure 1.26 an alert has been triggered by an image editing program trying to access the Internet. Although there is no obvious reason for such a program requiring the Internet, many programs these days use the Internet to regularly look for program updates. Operate the Yes button to permit Internet access or the No button to block it. Tick the checkbox if you would like this answer to be used automatically each time the program tries to access the Internet.

Sometimes the alert will genuinely find something that is amiss. In Figure 1.27 the alert shows that a file called msbb.exe has tried to access the Internet.

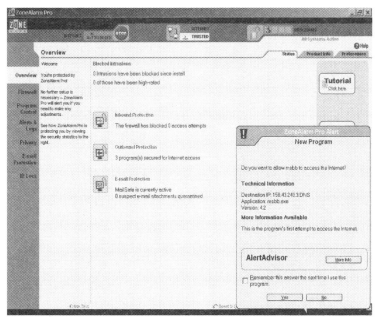

Fig.1.27 The alert was produced by an adware component

Some delving on the Internet revealed that this is part of the Ncase adware program, which was supposedly uninstalled from the PC a few weeks earlier. Clearly it had not been successfully uninstalled, and some further work was needed in order to banish it from the system.

Windows XP SP2

Service Pack 2 for Windows XP became available during the preparation of this book, and this represents an important step forward in computer

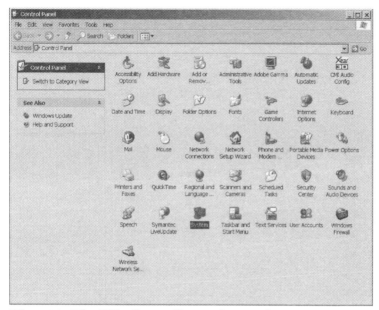

Fig.1.28 The Windows Control Panel

security. It addresses many of the so-called "security holes" that have been exploited by worms, viruses, etc., in recent times. If you are using a computer that was purchased recently it will probably have Service Pack 2 installed already.

It is easy to determine whether Service Pack 2 is installed, and the first step is to go to the Windows Control Panel (Figure 1.28). Access the control panel by choosing Settings and Control Panel from the Start menu. Then double-click the System icon and then operate the General tab in the new window that appears (Figure 1.29). If Service Pack 2 is installed, it will be mentioned in the System section of the page.

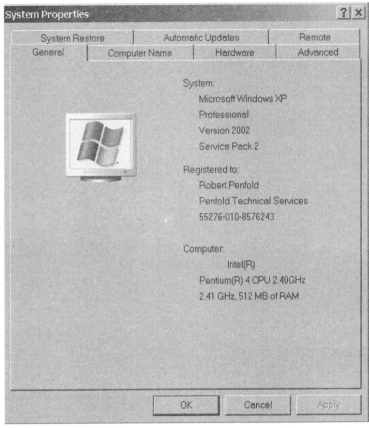

*Fig.1.29 The System section indicates that Service
Pack 2 is installed*

If you do not have Service Pack 2 installed then you
should certainly download and install it from the
Microsoft web site (www.micrsoft.com) or obtain the
CD-ROM version from Microsoft.

The original version of Windows XP has a built-in
firewall program, but it is rather basic and is not

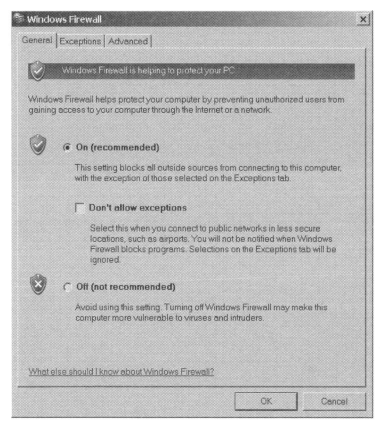

Fig.1.30 The firewall can be switched on and off, as required

activated by default. Consequently, it was easily overlooked and was not much used. The firewall program of Service Pack 2 is somewhat improved, and it is activated by default. Consequently, an alert will be provided when a program tries to activate the Internet for the first time. You then have the choice of allowing access or continuing to block access. Do

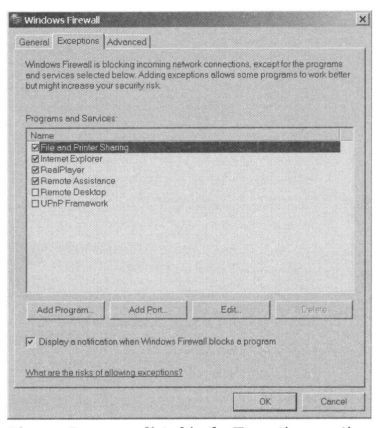

Fig.1.31 Programs listed in the Exceptions section

not permit a program to connect to the Internet unless you are sure that it is safe to do so.

It is possible to switch off the firewall, but this should only be done if another firewall is going to be installed. The firewall is controlled by double-clicking the Windows Firewall icon in the Control Panel, which produces the window of Figure 1.30. The radio buttons enable the firewall to be switched on or off, as

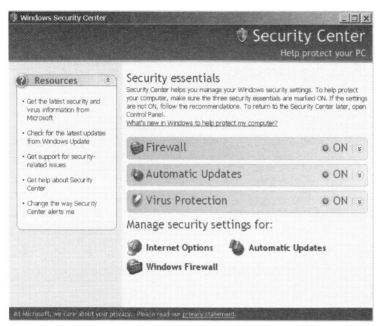

*Fig.1.32 The Security Center is a new addition
provided by Service Pack 2*

required. Operating the Exceptions tab produces a
window like the one shown in Figure 1.31. The main
part of the window lists the programs that the firewall
grants Internet access. Remove the tick from the
checkbox for any program that you would like to block.

The Windows Security Center (Figure 1.32) is a new
feature that is provided by Service Pack 2. It is
accessed by double-clicking the Security Center icon
in the Windows Control Panel. It uses a "traffic light"
system that will show three green lights if the firewall
is switched on, automatic updating of Windows is

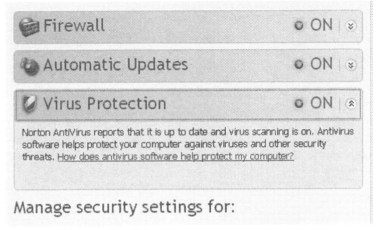

Fig.1.33   Here the Virus Protection section has been expanded to provide more information

active, and the computer is using a recognised antivirus program. A red light indicates that the relevant feature is not "alive and kicking". A yellow light will be produced if the state of a facility is indeterminate, such as when an antivirus program has been detected but its update status can not be read.

More information from any of the three sections can be obtained by left-clicking on the relevant section. A drop-down panel then provides further details. In Figure 1.33 the Virus Protection section has been expanded, and this shows that Norton Antivirus is installed and has indicated that it is up-to-date. Left-click an entry again in order to remove the drop-down panel.

Points to remember

The term "virus" tends to be used to describe a wide range of harmful files, but strictly speaking it refers to a specific type of threat. A virus attaches itself to other files and tries to spread across the system. It may or may not cause severe damage to the system, and in practice most viruses do try to damage data and (or) the operating system.

A Trojan is a program that purports to be one thing but is actually something else. Some Trojans attack the system, much like viruses, but can not replicate and spread like a virus. A backdoor Trojan helps hackers to penetrate your computer system, either with a view to causing damage or to steal information.

A worm looks for security "holes" in other systems in an attempt to attack that system and spread from it. Some of the worst computer attacks in recent times have been from worms that are spread by Emails, and replicate by sending copies of themselves to every address in the address book of the attacked system.

Prevention is better than cure. A good antivirus program can cost little or nothing and will immediately spot most viruses. New viruses are appearing all the time, so remember to keep the antivirus program up-to-date.

Antivirus programs are of limited use against hackers. In order to keep hackers at bay it is essential to use either a software or hardware firewall. Ideally, both should be used if you have some form of broadband connection, especially if it is of the "always on" variety.

Visiting dodgy sites and using "pirated" software are good ways of introducing viruses and other harmful files to your PC. Using peer-to-peer programs to swap files is another good way of doing it.

Use common sense and never take anything on the Internet at face value.

Antivirus software

Be prepared

Many computer users take the view that they do not need antivirus software until and unless a virus attacks their PC. This is a rather short-sighted attitude and one that is asking for trouble. By the time that you know a virus has infected your PC it is likely that a substantial amount of damage will have already been done to the system files and (or) your own data files. Using antivirus software to help sort out the mess after a virus has struck is "shutting the stable door after the horse has bolted". The virus may indeed be removed by the antivirus software, but there may be no way of correcting all the damage that has been done.

Another point to bear in mind is that your PC could be rendered unbootable by the virus. Many viruses attack the operating system and will try to make the system unbootable. If the system is not bootable, you can not install antivirus software. Actually, it might not be possible to install antivirus software even if the computer can be booted into Windows, and it would probably not be a good idea to do so anyway.

Most antivirus programs do some basic checks as part of the installation process. The program will not be installed if any hint of a virus is detected. The reason for this is that the installation process involves copying numerous files onto the hard disc and making changes to some of the Windows system files. This can provide an opportunity for the virus to spread and do further damage.

Many antivirus programs can be used once a virus has attacked a PC, and even if the PC can not be booted into Windows. One approach is to either have a set of boot floppy discs supplied as part of the package, or for these rescue discs to be produced during installation. If the PC becomes unbootable at some later date and a virus is thought to be the cause, the PC is booted from the first disc in the set. A series of checks are then performed, with the other discs being used as and when required.

A more modern alternative to this method is for the installation disc to be a boot type. The basic facilities provided are generally much the same as when using a set of boot discs, but there is no need to keep changing discs. Also, the high capacity of a CD-ROM means that more facilities are easily included in the program suite, if required. The drawback of both methods is that the discs will be something less than fully up-to-date, and may not be able to handle some of the more recent viruses.

Other options

There are other ways of handling things that do not involve any form of antivirus rescue disc. Where there is a recent backup of the system and all your data it makes sense to simply wipe the hard disc clean by reformatting it and then restoring the backup. This will completely destroy any infected files and should provide you with an infection-free system. However, in this situation it would be a good idea to run some antivirus scans on the restored system just in case the backup copy is infected. Remember that viruses are often designed to lay dormant for some time. The virus could have infected the PC many weeks prior to it showing any obvious signs of the infection.

Another approach is to again wipe the hard disc of all its contents but to then reinstall everything "from scratch". It is important to realise that with this method any data on the hard disc drive will be lost. Depending on the importance of the data on the disc, and whether backup copies are available, it might be necessary to rescue the data on the disc first, or to attempt a rescue anyway. It might not be possible to rescue anything in cases where the damage to the contents of the disc is severe. Unless you have a backup of the system there is no alternative to reinstalling everything "from scratch". Any data that has not been backed up will be lost, which is why you should always have at least one backup copy of any important data.

For those prepared to mess around with the hardware, another method is to add a hard disc to the PC. This disc is set as drive C (the boot disc) and it has Windows installed in the normal way, complete with some antivirus software. The original disc is used as drive D in the new setup, but it is not installed until everything has been fully installed on the new drive C. With this setup it is possible to boot into the fresh copy of Windows on drive C, run the antivirus software, and then use it to scan the infected drive D.

Provided the infected disc can be repaired, the hardware setup can be restored to its original configuration. If not, the new drive can be retained as the boot drive and the applications programs are installed onto it. Any undamaged data files can be copied from the old disc to the new one, and the old disc can then be reformatted. Either way the expense of the new hard disc is incurred, but you have an additional disc that can be more than a little useful for backup purposes.

A method that can not be wholeheartedly recommended is to remove the infected hard disc from the PC and set it to operate as drive D in another PC. The antivirus software on the other PC can then be used to scan the infected disc and, hopefully, produce a cure. There is nothing fundamentally wrong with this way of handling things, and it has a good chance of success. It is difficult to recommend it though, because there is a definite risk of the infection being spread to the second PC rather than being removed from the first one. I suppose that there is little to lose if the second PC is an old one that is not used in any serious applications, and it does not contain any important data. Other methods are preferable unless this is the case.

Adding hard disc drives or moving a hard drive to another PC is not something that can be recommended for those of limited experience. It is probably not a practical proposition for beginners unless a reasonably expert helper can be found. The only practical approaches for beginners are to clear the infection using antivirus software, or to restore a backup of the system if that method fails.

This chapter covers the use of antivirus software and similar programs that are designed to keep your PC clean of any form of infection. Correct use of the appropriate software does not guarantee that the operation of your PC will never be seriously disrupted by a virus or similar infection, but it does greatly reduce the chances of serious problem developing. Making and restoring a complete copy of a hard disc is covered in the final chapter.

Background

Software firewalls were considered in the previous chapter, and Zone Alarm Pro was used as an example of how these programs are set up and used. In order to perform its task properly a software firewall has to run as a background task, monitoring the Internet activity of the PC. With Zone Alarm Pro you have the option of bringing up the program window, but this is mainly done to alter the default settings or view the statistics generated by the program.

An antivirus program does not have to run as a background task, but it does have to do so in order to be as effective as possible. You could simply use the program to periodically scan the drives of your PC, and antivirus programs invariably have this mode of operation. In fact most can be set up to provide automatic scans at a certain time on a given day of each week.

This way of handling things has a big limitation though. It is possible for a virus to be on the system for nearly a week before the discs are scanned and there is any possibility of it being detected. In that time the virus could become well entrenched and would probably start to attack the files on the hard disc drive. More frequent scans could be scheduled, but the computer would then spend much of its time looking for viruses. This would probably be inconvenient, and would significantly reduce the operating life of the hard disc drive.

Most antivirus programs have two or three different modes of operation. In addition to the scanning mode, most can operate in real-time, and many have some form of rescue mode that tries to cure problems if a virus should find its way onto the hard disc. It is the real-time mode that is probably the most important. Like a firewall, the program runs in the background and monitors Internet activity. In fact most programs do rather more than that, and also monitor the interchangeable disc drives such as the floppy and CD-ROM drives.

The general idea is to have the program spot a virus as soon as it enters the system, and to then alert the user to its presence before it has time to spread. This greatly reduces the chances of the PC coming to grief, but there is a slight downside with both software firewalls and real-time antivirus programs. They both operate continuously in the background and utilise some of the computer's resources. In particular, they take up a certain amount of the PC's processing time and its memory. This tends to make the computer run applications programs a little slower.

In the past this problem was certainly more of an issue than it is now. The best PCs of ten years ago were far less powerful than an even an inexpensive PC of today. There was often a very marked loss of performance when a firewall or antivirus program was installed on a PC. These days it is unlikely that a noticeable reduction in performance will occur, but there will be some reduction in speed.

Another problem with many of the early antivirus programs was that they tended to take over the PC. Most were more than a little intrusive in operation, and some produced over-protective warnings whenever you tried to do practically anything. Fortunately, most modern antivirus programs are much more discreet and remain unseen in the background most of the time.

Real world programs

There are a number of "big name" antivirus programs, and any of these should provide your PC with excellent protection against viruses and other harmful files. These programs provide broadly the same functions but are different in points of detail. We will consider a few representative examples here. It is worth emphasising the point that it is not a good idea to have more than one of these programs installed on your PC at any one time. Antivirus programs are less intrusive than they used to be, but they still operate continuously in the background monitoring the PC's activity.

Having two of the programs operating simultaneously can produce conflicts that can easily result in the PC crashing. With many of the older antivirus programs you never actually managed to get that far. Having two of them installed on a PC usually resulted in it failing to boot into Windows. It might seem reasonable to have two or three antivirus programs installed, since this gives a better chance of a virus being detected. In practice it does not work very well when

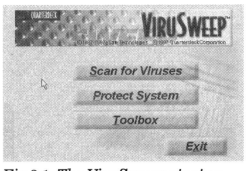

Fig.2.1   The ViruSweep startup screen

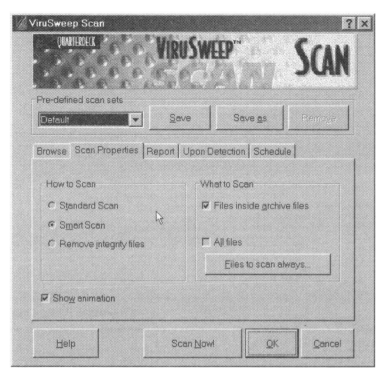

Fig.2.2 The first ViruSweep screen after scanning for viruses

applied to real-time monitoring. It can be useful to have the ability to scan using two or three antivirus programs in succession, but having more than one operating at a time is definitely something to be avoided.

Figure 2.1 shows the startup screen for the Quarterdeck ViruSweep program, and operating the "Scan For Viruses" button takes the user into further screens that permit various options to be selected. The first screen (Figure 2.2) permits the user to select

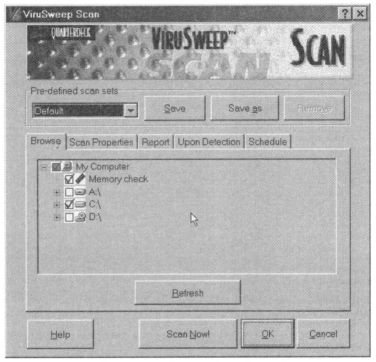

Fig.2.3 Here the type of scan is selected

the parts of the system that will be checked. Viruses can exist in memory as well as in disc files, so checking the memory is normally an option. Further screens enable the type of scan to be selected (Figure 2.3), and the action to be taken if a virus is detected (Figure 2.4). Most anti-virus software has the option of removing a virus rather than simply indicating that it has been detected. Note though, that in some cases it might not be possible to automatically "kill" a virus. The program will then usually give details of how to manually remove the virus.

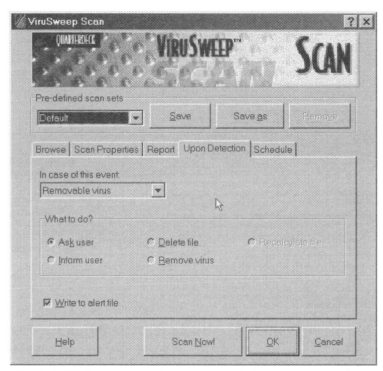

Fig.2.4 This screen gives control over the action taken when a virus is detected

Things are likely to be very difficult if you do not use anti-virus software and your PC becomes infected. On the face of it, you can simply load an anti-virus program onto the hard disc and then use it to remove the virus. As explained previously, it is definitely not advisable to try this method, and most software of this type will not load onto the hard disc if it detects that a virus is present. There would be a very real danger of the antivirus program itself spreading the infection and becoming damaged itself.

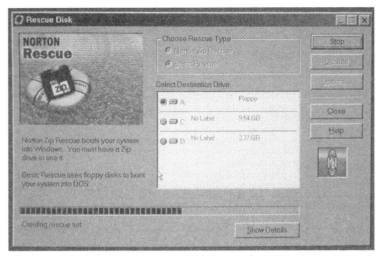

Fig.2.5 Making recovery discs using Norton AV

Boot disc

The method offered by many (but not all) anti-virus suites is to boot from a special floppy disc that contains anti-virus software. With this method there is no need to load any software onto the hard disc, and consequently there is no risk of the anti-virus software causing the virus to be spread further over the system. With the Norton Antivirus program a boot disc plus four support discs are made during the installation process (Figure 2.5). If boot problems occur at a later date, the PC can be booted using the Norton boot disc, and with the aid of the other discs a comprehensive range of virus scans can be undertaken (Figure 2.6). In some cases the virus can be removed automatically, and it might also be possible to have any damage to the system files repaired automatically as well.

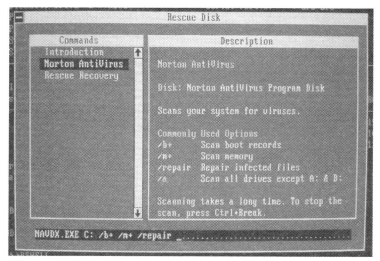

Fig.2.6 Virus scanning using the recovery discs

Free check-up

Antivirus software does not rate as one of the more expensive types, and a good antivirus program can be quite inexpensive. It does not have to cost anything at all and there are various free options available if you would prefer not to buy one of the mainstream commercial products. The best source for this type of software is undoubtedly the cover-mounted discs provided "free" with computer magazines. There seems to be a steady stream of antivirus software provided on these discs. Some of these programs are actually only time-limited trials that are of no use for long-term use.

There is a catch with many of the others in that the program is free, but a subscription has to be paid in order to keep the virus database up to date. Note

2   Antivirus software

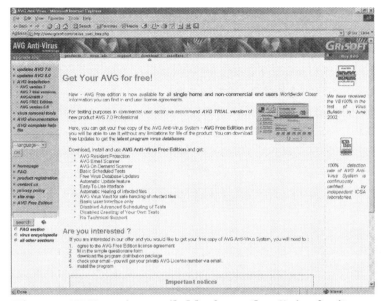

Fig.2.7 AVG 6.0 is available from the Grisoft site

that even with full commercial products the updates
are usually only available free of charge for one year.
After that time you either have to buy the new version
of the program of subscribe to updates. Of course,
you can simply continue to use out of date antivirus
software, and it will still detect many viruses.
However, if a new virus infects your PC it is unlikely
that an out of date antivirus will be able to detect it.

There are one or two totally free antivirus programs
available on the Internet, where you do not even have
to pay for monthly online updates to the database.
AVG 6.0 from Grisoft is one that is certainly worth
trying. The Grisoft site is at:

www.grisoft.com

68

On the home page there should be a link in the list down the left-hand side called something like "AVG Free Edition". Activating this link will bring up a page like the one in Figure 2.7. This gives some information about the free version of the AVG anti-virus program and provides a link that enables it to be downloaded. You do have to go through a registration process, but it is worth the effort. Monthly updates to AVG are available free of charge. This program has a reputation for being very efficient, and it certainly detected a couple of backdoor Trojan programs on my system that a certain well-known commercial program had failed to detect. It is one of the best freebies on the Internet.

It does have one major limitation, which is that it does not have a rescue mode of the type provided by Norton Antivirus and some other programs. There is a facility to backup important system files so that they can be restored if the originals become damaged by a virus. There is no facility to boot from a floppy disc or CD-ROM drive and run virus checks. The program works effectively in the background detecting the vast majority of viruses, Trojans, etc., so there is little likelihood of a rescue mode being required. However, if you should get unlucky it might be necessary to resort to another antivirus program in order to clear an infection.

AVG does have a useful range of facilities and in other respects it is a very capable program. In common with most antivirus programs you can set it to scan the system on a regular basis, and it also has an

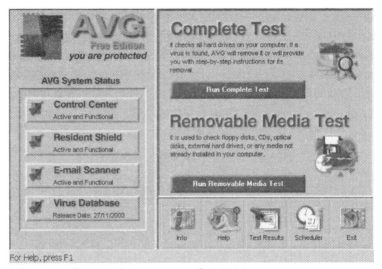

Fig.2.8   The main screen of AVG 6.0

automatic update facility.   Manual scanning is also available, and this is another standard feature for this type of software.   If you suspect that there might be a virus infection somewhere in the PC you can get the program to do a complete scan of the entire system. Another standard option is to scan one or more of the interchangeable disc drives such as a floppy or CD-ROM drive.   This is useful in cases where you suspect that a disc someone has given you might contain a virus.

AVG normally runs automatically at start-up and then runs in the background until the PC is shut down, but it can be started in the normal way from the Start menu.   It then appears in a window like the one shown in Figure 2.8.   One of the large buttons gives access

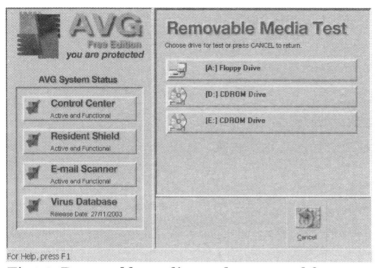

*Fig.2.9 Removable media can be scanned for
          viruses*

to the full system scan and the lower one permits the removable media to be checked. Operating the lower button changes the window to look something like Figure 2.9, which has a button for each removable disc fitted to the computer. Operating one of the buttons runs a check on the appropriate drive, and a window showing the results (Figure 2.10) is produced when the process has been completed.

The test results will show what action was taken if one or more viruses were detected. The action taken depends on how the program is set up and precisely what it finds. It will leave the infected file unchanged, delete it, or quarantine the file by moving to the secure folder that is called the "Virus Vault" in AVG terminology. Alternatively, it will do nothing and ask the user to select the required option.

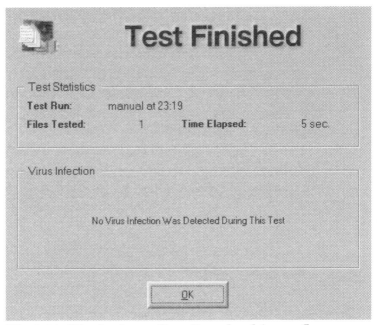

*Fig.2.10 The test results after checking a floppy
           disc*

When running in the background the program is
represented by a small button on the toolbar at the
bottom of the Windows desktop. Double-clicking the
button brings up the control window of Figure 2.11,
and this is typical of the way antivirus programs
operate. Using this it is possible to alter a number of
settings, including the types of scan that are provided.
Unless there is good reason to do otherwise it is
probably best to leave the default settings. It is
definitely not a good idea to reduce the types of scan
that are provided since this could obviously leave
security holes in the system.

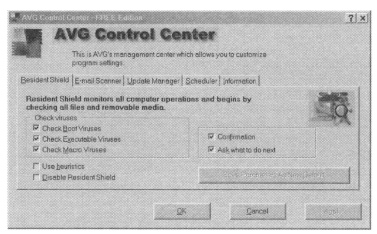

Fig.2.11   The AVG Control Center

Online scan

There are various companies that offer online virus scanning facilities, and most of these are free. Although online scanning might seem an attractive option in cases where a PC has a virus infection but you have no antivirus software, there is a drawback to their use in this situation. Obviously the PC must be largely operational before it can go online and be used with this type of scanning. Assuming it can get that far, the main problem is that online scanning is not exactly online scanning.

The name suggests that a program running at the server scans your PC for viruses, but in most cases very little of the software runs at the other end of the Internet link. The usual arrangement is for an antivirus program to be downloaded to your PC, temporarily installed, run, and then erased. The

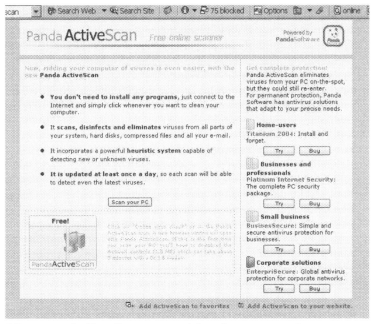

Fig.2.12 ActiveScan provides free scanning

problem with this method is that it is not really much different to installing an antivirus program and running it in the usual way. The file copying provides opportunities for any virus to propagate, and going online provides spyware and backdoor Trojans with an opportunity to "do their thing".

If you suspect that there could be a problem with a virus but have no definite proof, then it might be worth the risk if you do not have a better alternative. Online testing is also worthwhile if you do not intend to use normal antivirus software, but it is certainly not a genuine alternative to normal antivirus software. A program such as AVG 6.0 will monitor your PC and

Fig.2.13 The initial explanatory window

provide real-time protection. Any virus entering the system is likely to be detected immediately. With occasional online scanning there could be a significant gap between the infection occurring and the virus being detected. Even a few days or hours could be long enough for the virus to spread and damage your files.

I suppose online testing might be worthwhile if you are at the stage where you are desperate enough to try anything, but as far as possible it is best to avoid getting into that situation. Installing a free antivirus program on your PC is far better than getting into difficulties and then trying to recover the situation.

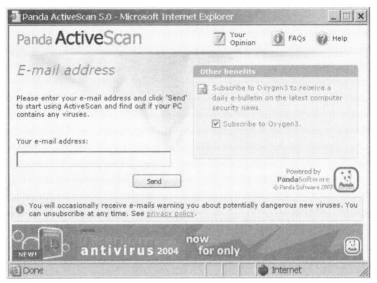

Fig.2.14 An Email address must be provided

An important point if you do try online virus scanning is to make sure that you use the services of a reputable company. In the early days of computer viruses it was quite common for infections to be spread via antivirus software that was actually a Trojan. This method has rather gone out of fashion, but the possibility of someone coming up with an online version can not be ruled out. Only using the services of a "big name" company should ensure that the scanning detects and removes any viruses rather than adding a few!

Panda Software is well known for its security oriented software suites, and they offer online scanning in the form of the ActiveScan facility (Figure 2.12). Operating the Scan Your PC link brings up the initial

Fig.2.15 Your location is also required

window of Figure 2.13, which briefly explains what
ActiveScan does. Operating the Next button moves
things on to the window of Figure 2.14 where you have
to enter your Email address. If you do not wish to
use your normal Email address for this type of thing
it is just a matter of setting up an account with
Hotmail, Yahoo, or one of the other online Email
providers. This account can then be used when
obtaining free online services, which almost
invariably require a valid Email address.

At the next window (Figure 2.15) you have to state
your country and (possibly) area within that country.
Things then move on to the stage where the software
is downloaded, and the security warning of Figure 2.16
might appear. Operate the Yes button to go ahead

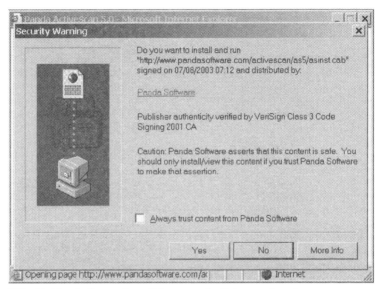

*Fig.2.16 A download is needed in order to carry
out the scan*

with the download. The window of Figure 2.17
appears once the program has been downloaded and
temporarily installed. The buttons near the top left-
hand corner of the screen enable various parts of the
system to be tested, and for this example the All My
Computer option was used. The checkboxes in the
right-hand section of the window give some control
over the type of scan that is undertaken. You can opt
to have Trojans neutralised for example.

A window like the one in Figure 2.18 is produced once
the scan is under way. This has a bargraph display to
show how far the scan has progressed. A table of
results is included, and this shows things like the
number of files tested, and any actions taken by the

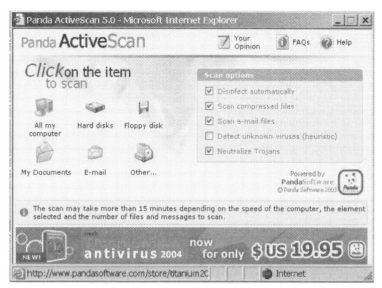

Fig.2.17 Select the required type of scan

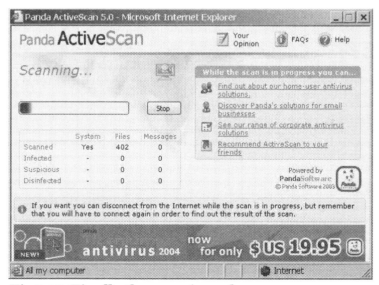

Fig.2.18 Finally the scan is under way

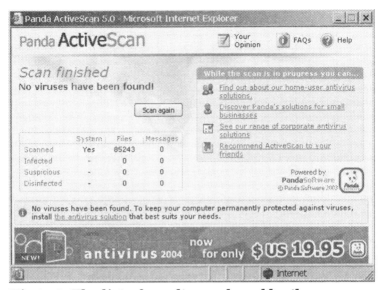

Fig.2.19 The list of results produced by the scan

program. Note that it is not necessary to remain online while the scanning takes place, but that the PC must be online before the final results can be produced. As with any antivirus scanning, it can take some time if there is a large and largely full hard disc drive to check. Eventually the scan will be completed though (Figure 2.19) and a full set of results will then be shown.

The program is much like an ordinary antivirus program in operation, and this is essentially what it is. However, when you exit the program it will effectively be uninstalled, and it can not be run in the usual fashion.

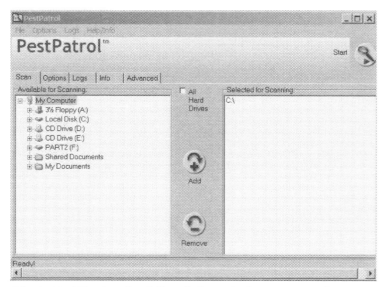

Fig.2.20 First select the drives to be scanned

Non-virus

Antivirus programs, as their name suggests, are primarily concerned with the detection and removal of viruses. Most will actually detect a wider range of threats, including most Trojans, spyware, and backdoor Trojans. How well these types of threat are detected varies somewhat from one program to another. Antivirus programs are not usually designed to detect what could be termed nuisance programs, such as adware programs and their related files. However, there are programs that are designed to deal with this type of thing, and they will mostly detect some of the more serious threats such as spyware.

Pest Patrol is one of the best known programs of this type, and it is the one that will be used as the basis of

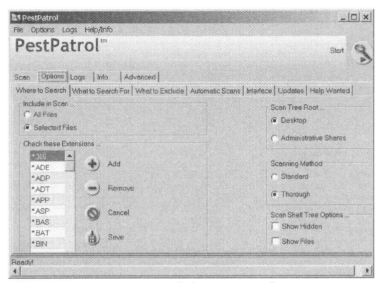

*Fig.2.21 You can control the type and
thoroughness of the scan*

this example. The initial screen of Pest Patrol is
shown in Figure 2.20, and the first task is to select the
drives that will be scanned. This is just a matter of
selecting the required drives in the panel on the left
using the standard Windows methods. The Add
button is then left-clicked in order to add the drives
to the list in the right panel. A drive can be removed
from the list by selecting its entry and operating the
Remove button. Simply tick the checkbox if you wish
to check all the hard drives.

Operating the Options tab produces a further row of
tabs, and these give access to a range of options that
control the way Pest Patrol scans the disc. There are
standard and thorough options for example (Figure

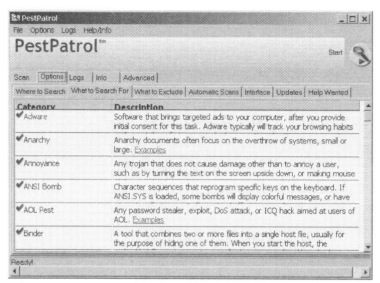

Fig.2.22 You can control the types of "pest" that the program seeks

2.21), and you can also set the program to only look for certain types of "pest" (Figure 2.22). It is by no means essential to do any "fine tuning" though, and the program should work well enough if it scans the discs using the default settings. To go ahead with a scan it is just a matter of operating the Start button in the top right-hand corner of the window.

You are presented with a scrollable list of results once Pest Patrol has finished the scan (Figure 2.23). It is essential to look down the list, item by item, even in cases where there are a large number of entries. What you and Pest Patrol consider to be "pests" could be rather different. Remember that removing adware files could result in any programs supported by that

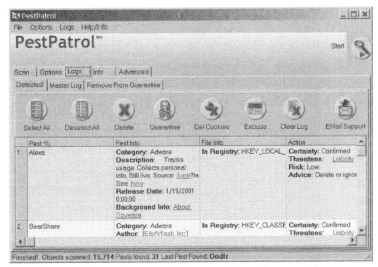

Fig.2.23 A list of "pests" is produced once the scan has been completed

adware becoming inoperative. You are unlikely to get away with installing supported software, disabling the associated adware, and then continuing to use the supported software. Blocking adware with a firewall does sometimes leave the supported application fully operational, but this is a morally dubious practice.

Having decided the fate of the various entries, it is just a matter of selecting each batch and then operating the appropriate button. In this example none of the detected files were required, so they were all deleted. The list changes to show what has been done to each file (Figure 2.24). Note that the program may be unable to delete some files and folders. It will then show the location of the relevant files or folders and recommend manual deletion.

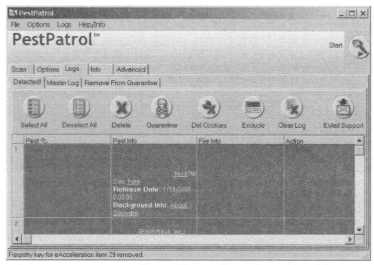

Fig.2.24 Pest Patrol confirms that the offending files have been deleted

Email scams

The advice about Emails used to be along the lines that there is no risk from a simple text Email, and that the real threat from Emails comes from attachments that are not what they are supposed to be. These days it is necessary for this type of advice to be heavily qualified, since many Email problems now stem from the text contained in an Email. To be brutally frank, in many cases the problems also stem from the naivety of the recipients. It is essential for anyone receiving Emails to act as the main defence against the various scams and hoaxes that are becoming increasingly common.

The subject of hoax viruses was covered in chapter 1. This type of hoax is not exclusive to Emails, but this method of transmission is used for practically all hoax viruses. If someone sends you an Email saying that they have accidentally sent a virus to you in an Email or attachment, do some checking to ensure that there really is a virus. When someone sent a hoax virus to my sister suggesting that a couple of files needed to be erased in order to eradicate it, about 30 seconds of checking on the Internet was sufficient to establish that it was indeed a hoax. Remember that it is unwise to trust this type of thing simply because the Email carries a sender's address that you know. The sender's address could be about as genuine as the virus, and there is also the possibility that the sender has been fooled and is unwittingly spreading the hoax.

Email scams have been on the increase in recent years. The first one to come to fame was the Nigerian scam where you pay money to help a Nigerian business man to get his money out of the country. In return for your help you supposedly get large sums of money, but there is no prize for guessing how much you actually get back. There is no prize either with another common scam where you are told that you have won a competition but you need to pay a fee in order to get the prize. Usually there is no prize, but occasionally there is a worthless prize. This scam is just the Email equivalent of one that will be familiar to recipients of ordinary junk mail.

A more recent and potentially costly scam is where an Email is received from a financial organisation of some kind. Yahoo's PayPal system for transferring funds was the first to be targeted, but several online banks were targeted later. The Email asks you to sign in at the site and confirm your password and other details. There is a link on the Email that leads to what looks very much like the real site, and the address is very similar to the real thing. However, the link actually leads to a fake site where you give away your account details if you sign in and provide the requested information.

So far this scam has not been particularly successful. Most recipients of the Emails realised that there was something amiss and either ignored or reported it. Others ignored the link and went to the relevant page in the usual way, thus avoiding the fake site. To avoid anything of this type it is just a matter of not supplying passwords or any other sensitive information in answer to Emails or telephone calls. As many online organisations go to great lengths to point out, they will never ask you for your password.

This general type of scam is not really all that new. Some Internet service providers (ISPs) and AOL in particular, used to have problems with new users getting communications of one type or another asking them to confirm their passwords. The crooks were trying to get the passwords so that they could obtain Internet access at the expense of the legitimate user. This practice died out due to changes in the way that Internet access is provided, but it does demonstrate the point that you should never divulge passwords for any Internet service, not just the financial variety.

Attachments

Although they are not the only threat, attachments remain the most likely route for a serious Email attack. In recent years a number of Email viruses have rapidly spread around the world. These Email viruses utilise the automation features that are built into Microsoft Office and other programs. These facilities are intended to provide a means of doing clever things that make life easier for users, but they can also hand over control of the PC to a virus.

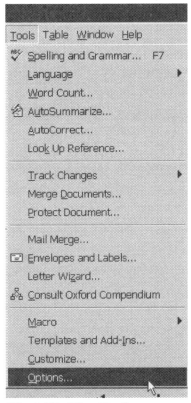

Fig.2.25 The Tools menu

If you do not need these facilities, disabling them is a simple but effective means of removing this threat to your PC. Microsoft has a useful download for Outlook 98 and 2000 that provides protection against viruses such as ILOVEYOU and Melissa. It disables the ability to download attachments that could contain a virus. The download and further information are

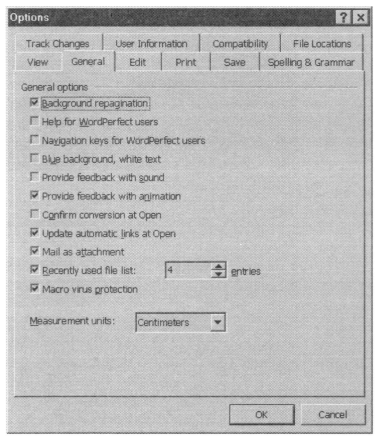

*Fig.2.26 Make sure that the box for Macro Virus
Protection is ticked*

available from this web page:

http://office.microsoft.com/downloads/2000/
Out2ksec.aspx

Another tactic is to turn off the automatic running of
scripts in Word, Access, and Excel. First select
Options from the tools menu (Figure 2.25), and then

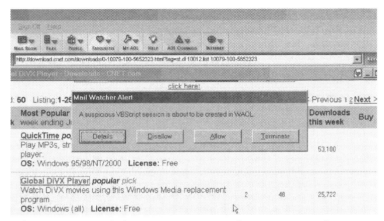

Fig.2.27 Suspicious events produce a warning

operate the General tab in the window that appears (Figure 2.26). Make sure that the checkbox for Macro virus protection is ticked.

It makes sense to have the security settings of Internet Explorer as high as possible, or failing that as high as possible without preventing the programs from providing the functions you require. Adjusting these settings was covered in the previous chapter so it will not be covered again here. This is a simple aspect of Internet security that many users seem to overlook, so make sure that you use the most secure settings that do not block or seriously hinder the facilities you wish to use.

Email antivirus

There are protection programs designed specifically to deal with Email viruses and other infections carried by scripts. Obviously this type of program has to run

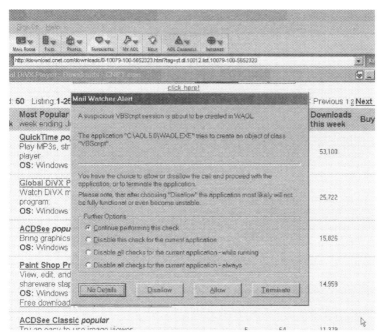

Fig.2.28 More details of the current operation can be obtained

in real-time, and it produces a warning if it detects something suspicious happening. Figure 2.27 shows a warning message produced by Mail Watcher from Computer Associates, which detects attempts to access the Email system. Since many of the events detected by the program are perfectly legitimate it does not block them, but instead provides a simple control panel. The Terminate button is pressed if it is felt that the detected action is possibly a virus. Operating the Allow button enables things to proceed normally. Left-clicking the Details button opens a new window (Figure 2.28) that gives more details of the current operation and the options for dealing with it.

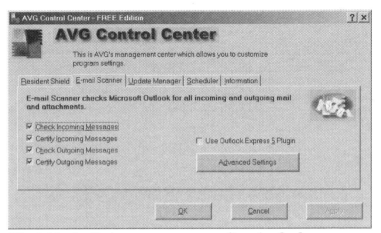

*Fig.2.29 Antivirus programs often include an
Email scanning facility*

Most antivirus suites now include a program that can
check Emails or have this facility built into the main
program. AVG 6.0 has a built-in Email scanning
facility, and it is possible to select the required checks
from the Email section of its Control Center (Figure
2.29). This type of thing is fine if you are using Outlook
or Outlook Express as the Email client, but these days
many people use Internet based Email services such
as those provided by Hotmail or the Yahoo!. These
do not usually make use of Outlook, Outlook Express,
or any similar program, but instead have their
facilities built into the system. An antivirus program
such as AVG does not usually provide any protection
with a fully Internet based Email service.

This is not to say that no protection is available for
users of these services. Some Email service
providers have facilities for checking attachments

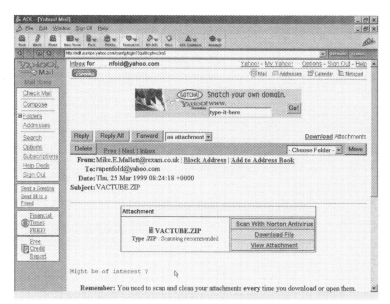

Fig.2.30 This Email has a ZIP file attachment

prior to downloading them. Figure 2.30 shows an
Email that is being viewed using the Yahoo.com Email
service. This has a ZIP file attachment and one option
for dealing with the attachment is to simply download
it regardless of the risk. Another option is to scan it
using the system's built-in Norton antivirus program.
The scanning process is very rapid because the file
is being checked while it is still on the server. The
Email, complete with its attachment, can be erased
if a problem is discovered. In this way the file never
reaches your PC and can not infect it. Usually
everything will be all right and a reassuring message
will appear (Figure 2.31).

A third option is available, and this enables the
attachment to be viewed so that you can check that it

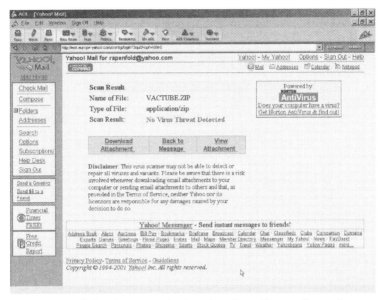

Fig.2.31 This time no infection has been found

is genuine and not an impostor. Obviously this is not of much use with all types of file, but it is useful with something like a Word DOC file that could contain a macro virus. The system will accurately interpret the document so that it appears much the same as it would when viewed using Word itself (Figure 2.32). This method does not guarantee that the attachment is virus-free, but you can at least check that it is a proper document from someone you know.

If you need to work on the document in Word it must be downloaded, but this is not necessary if you only need to read its contents. Having viewed and read the contents the Email and attachment can be deleted. Another possibility is to cut and paste the

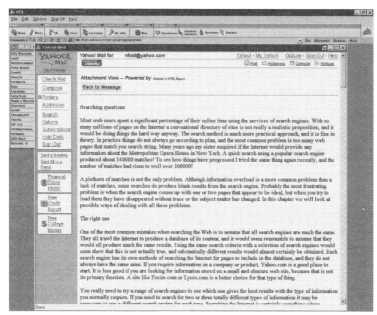

Fig.2.32 A Word file in the viewer program

text from the Email viewer to Word. Select the required text and press the Control and C keys to copy the text to the clipboard. Open Word and then press the Control and V keys to copy the text into Word from the clipboard. With this method any clever tricks in the original document will be lost, but so will any macro virus.

If you need to exchange formatted text documents via Email attachments it is worth considering the rich text format. Documents in this format can have the usual types of Windows formatting including alignment, different fonts, text colours, etc. It does not support any type of macro language, so files that use this format can not contain a macro virus. Plain text files are also safe, but have no formatting capability. Of course, these files are only safe when they are what they purport to be. Any data file needs to be checked for authenticity before you download it.

Many people now take the "belt and braces" approach of simply refusing to open any Email attachments. I suppose that this is a practical approach for anyone that has no real need to exchange anything other than plain text by Email, but it is not practical if you need to receive images, formatted documents, etc., via this route.

It still makes sense not to open attachments if you do not know the sender and (or) are not expecting an Email with an attachment. Where necessary, check that the Email and attachment genuinely come from the supposed sender, and only open the attachment once you have verified their authenticity. Unfortunately, these days anything received via Email has to be treated with a degree of suspicion.

Internet resource

When dealing with a computer virus remember that the Internet carries a vast amount of information about dealing with many viruses and other forms of infection.   Some of the information is general in nature, but there is also a large amount of information about specific viruses. This can be very useful where you know that a PC is infected with a certain virus but you are having difficulties in dealing with it. Using

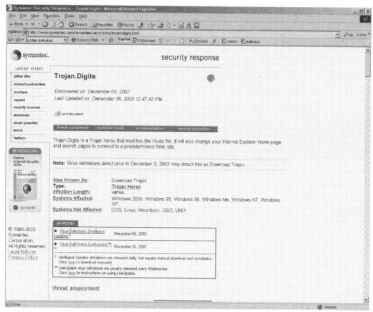

Fig.2.33 The Symantec site has lots of useful information about viruses

the name of the virus in a search engine, perhaps with the words "computer" and "virus", should produce some helpful information. There might even be a utility program that helps to remove the virus and repair damaged files.

As always though, proceed with caution and as far as possible stick with the sites of well-known companies. The Symantec site (www.symantec.com) contains a great deal of information about numerous viruses (Figure 2.33). Details of newly discovered viruses are given prominence on this site, and the sites of the other companies involved in producing antivirus software.

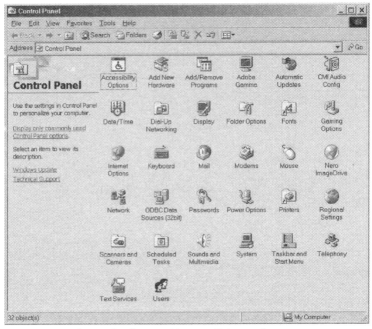

Fig.2.34 The Windows Control Panel

Manual removal

When some form of infection occurs on a PC there is a natural tendency to look for a program that will remove it for you. Being realistic about it, a program such as a virus or Trojan is not going to be removable via the normal route, because it will not install itself into Windows as a normal program. It will do its best to stay hidden, and you will probably need some help in order to locate and remove the relevant file or files. With some of the more minor problems it is not necessary to resort to some form of antivirus or "pest control" program.

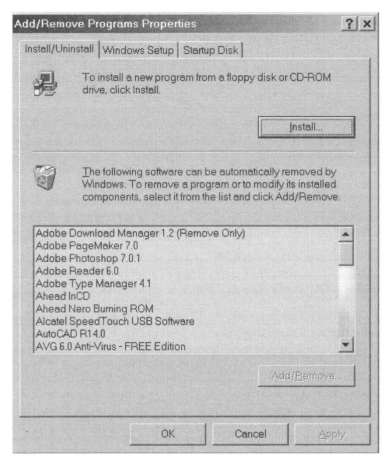

Fig.2.35 A list of all the installed programs is provided

For example, many adware programs are installed without it being made clear to the user that they are being added to the system, but most of them are installed in the normal way. Consequently, they can be uninstalled in the usual way. This means going to Settings in the Start menu and selecting Control Panel in the submenu that appears. The exact appearance of the Control Panel depends on how the computer is setup up, but it will probably look something like Figure 2.34. Double-click the Add/Remove Programs icon or text entry, as appropriate.

This launches a new window like the one of Figure 2.35, which includes a scrollable list of all the programs installed on the computer. Look down this to see if the program that is giving problems is installed, or if there is anything that should not be there. To uninstall a program it is necessary to first left-click its entry in the list to select it. Then operate the Add/Remove button and go through the additional steps needed to remove the program. These tend to be slightly different from one program to another, but it is usually just a matter of confirming that you wish to remove the program.

In the case of adware it is likely that there will be a warning to the effect that the software it supports will not operate properly if the program is removed. Unfortunately, in most cases the supported program will not be named, but you will probably be able to deduce this for yourself. It is up to you whether to remove the program anyway or put up with it. You might get a warning message saying that shared files are no longer needed by other applications and asking whether you wish to remove them. In theory it should be all right to operate the Yes button, but the No button is the safer option. Leaving shared files in place should still result in the program being properly uninstalled and rendered inoperative.

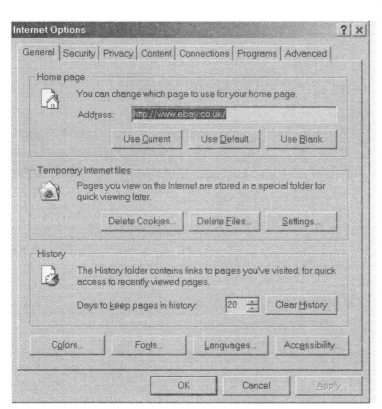

Fig.2.36 The homepage is easily changed

Some web sites play clever tricks that alter the home page of your browser. Each time the browser is launched you typically find either a pornography site or some form of directory or search engine. In most cases it is possible to set the homepage back to its original setting using the normal facilities of the browser. In the case of Internet Explorer select Internet Options from the Tools menu when running the program of from the Windows Control Panel.

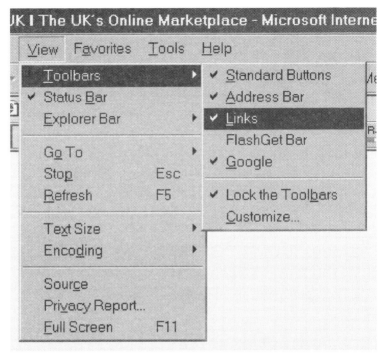

Fig.2.37 Toolbars are easily turned on and off

Either way a window like the one shown in Figure 2.36 will appear. Simply change the text in the Address textbox to the required web address.

Sometimes you can find that the homepage address keeps reverting to the one you have just removed. There can also be problems with a new toolbar appearing, often offering something like a search facility for pornography sites. A toolbar can be switched off by going to the View menu and selecting Toolbars (Figure 2.37). Find the offending toolbar in the list and remove the tick next to its name. This

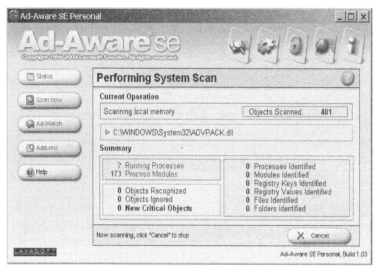

Fig.2.38 Ad-Aware SE carrying out a scan

should suppress it, but it does not remove the toolbar from the system.

In theory a toolbar should have an entry in the Add/ Remove Programs window, but one added to the system without your consent is unlikely to make itself as easy to remove as this. With a computer running under Windows ME or XP it is worth using the System Restore facility to take the system back a day or two. It is assumed here that the offending toolbar or homepage change entered the system within the last day or two. Taking the system settings back a couple of days should undo the changes and leave the system as it was previously. There is no guarantee that this will work or that no re-infection will occur, but in most cases it seems to do the trick. Note that any changes

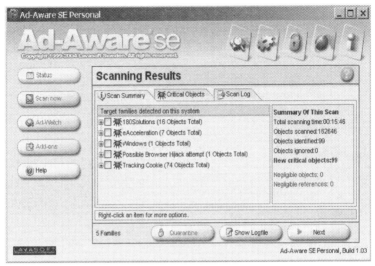

Fig.2.39 The results of the scan

you have made to the system within the last couple of days will also be undone and will have to be reinstated. Using the System Restore facility is covered in more detail in a later chapter.

Ad-Aware Personal

For persistent advert related problems it is well worth trying Ad-Aware SE Personal, which is a free download provided the program is for personal use. It can be downloaded from the Lavasoft web site (www.lavasoftusa.com), and the program file is only about 2.5 megabytes. It scans the files on the hard disc (Figure 2.38), including the Windows Registry files. The Registry is where many of the more persistent adware pests seem to be lodged. It then

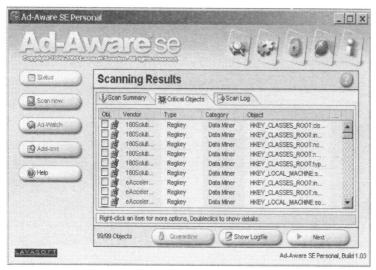

Fig.2.40 More detailed information is available

provides a general list of results (Figure 2.39), but more details are available for each section if required (Figure 2.40).

Where a computer has been used a great deal for surfing it is likely that the scan will produce a large number of results. Most of these are probably of no real consequence, but with luck the troublesome adware will have been located. To remove items it is just a matter of ticking their checkboxes and operating the Next button. They are then deleted or quarantined, and a summary of the cleanup operation is provided (Figure 2.41). In this example I simply had the program deal with everything it had found, which is usually the best course of action.

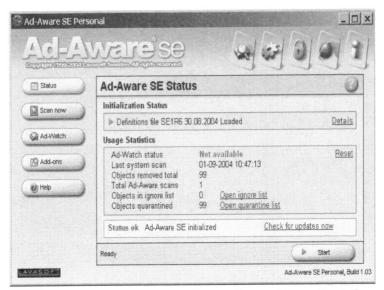

Fig.2.41 A status screen shows the actions that the program has performed

Points to remember

It is important to have antivirus software installed on a PC before it succumbs to an infection. Installing antivirus software on an infected PC is inadvisable because it entails file copying and changes to system files. Both of these can help a virus to spread across the hard disc drive. With good antivirus software installed it is unlikely that a virus will manage to take hold in the first place.

Some antivirus suites include a set of bootable floppy discs or a bootable CD-ROM so that antivirus checks can be made on a PC that does not have antivirus software installed. Using this type of software, checks can be made on a PC even if it can not be booted into Windows. One drawback of this method is that the antivirus software will not be fully up-to-date.

Antivirus software usually scans for more than viruses, and other harmful files such as Trojans and spyware will usually be found. Things such as adware will not be detected though, as they are often installed legitimately. Programs such as Pest Patrol will scan for adware and the like, and will remove them if required.

Provided you are using up to date software there should be no risk of you PC being infected if you open and read an Email. Attachments are a different matter, and are now a common means of trying to spread viruses.

Do not take Emails at face value, even if they supposedly come from an address that you normally deal with. With the aid of some common sense you have to act as the first line of defence against malicious and scam Emails.

Where possible, check your Email attachments for viruses before downloading them to your PC. Never open Email attachments if the sender is unknown to you, or you are not expecting a file to come from that particular person. You can always Email the supposed sender of the file to check its authenticity.

Programs for scanning Emails are available and this facility is included in many antivirus suites. These programs work with Outlook and Outlook Express but do not normally work with fully Internet based Email services. However, these services sometimes have built-in virus scanning facilities.

Spam, spam, spam

Is it spam?

Email has become one of the main ways in which PCs are attacked with some form of virus, worm, or whatever. Some aspects of Email security, such as phishing and the risks involved with attachments, were covered in the two previous chapters. This chapter deals with the increasingly thorny topic junk Emails, or "spam" as it is generally called these days.

Some say that the term "spam" is a contraction of "spurious advertising material", but the more generally accepted explanation is that it is derived from a Monty Python sketch. If you have an Email address then it is odds on that you receive at least a small amount of spam. It is quite likely that you receive large amounts of it every day. In fact spam now accounts for more than half the Emails sent, and spam is still on the increase. This has sparked very real fears that the Email system or even the Internet as a whole could eventually be brought to a virtual standstill by the sheer volume of junk Emails.

It would perhaps be a good idea to define exactly what is meant by spam, since this term does not really cover every type of advert sent via Email. Some people do interpret it this way, but this is a mistake. If you deal with companies via Email, advertising Emails they send you will probably not count as spam. It is likely you will have agreed to accept Email promotional material from these companies, and it is therefore perfectly acceptable for them to send you this type of material via an Email.

EU law has changed recently, and it is now illegal to send spam from within EU countries unless the recipient has given their consent. It is no longer acceptable for an EU based company to send Email advertisements unless you have specifically asked to receive them. Consequently, you should not receive Emails from an EU company simply because you have dealt with them in the past. However, if you opted for Emails when filling in an online order form or when registering with the company, then it is perfectly acceptable for them to send you Emails.

Most of the spam received by a typical Email account is the real thing, and it is unsolicited material from companies the account holder has never dealt with. The larger Email account providers such as Hotmail and Yahoo! have systems that try to block the more obvious batches of spam. In the past it was common for spammers to send their material to a range of Email addresses, trying every possible address in that range. Of course, most of the names did not match up with an account at Hotmail, Yahoo!, or whatever provider was under attack. Some would match an actual account though, and the cheapness of mass

Emailing is such that the small percentage of successes made the enterprise worthwhile. These days the Email companies have systems that soon block this sort of thing and block further Emails from that source.

Other methods are used in an attempt to filter junk Emails. If an address is used to send Emails it is likely that it will soon be put on a blacklist and blocked. This makes life difficult for the spammers, but it does not halt their activities. Spam is often sent via a hijacked computer system. Before too long the owner of the system will notice the attack and take counter measures, or the hijacked address will be blocked by the Email companies. The spammer then moves on to another system, and so it goes on.

Hijacked systems

A variation on the hijacked system is to use a spoof Email program together with either a genuine or fictitious "from" address on the junk Emails. The idea is for the program generating the spoof Emails to make it appear as though they are coming from another source. Usually the Email addresses used as the source are not genuine, but occasionally the address used is real.

This is probably by accident rather than design, but it is unfortunate for the owner of the Email address. They often get large numbers of complaints about spam that they have not actually sent. Apparently some users have abandoned Email addresses due to this problem. The advantage of this system for the spammers is that it is very easy to switch from one dummy source address to another, making it more difficult for automatic filtering to deal with the junk Emails produced.

Another technique used for filtering spam is to look for a particular set of words in the title of Emails. Junk Emails tend to promote a relatively limited range of products, such as get rich quick schemes, devices or drugs to make bits of your body get bigger, pornographic web sites, and medicines without a prescription. The same words therefore tend to turn up in the title fields of the junk Emails, and the filtering systems search for them. The spammers answer to this is to deliberately misspell words or use extra spaces so that "sex" could appear as "s e x" for example. Another ploy is to use odd terminology. This might get the spam through automatic filtering systems, but it does at least make the junk Emails easier for recipients to spot.

Spam senders are aware that most people will scan the contents of their Inbox in an attempt to identify the junk Emails so that they can be deleted without ever opening them. Many spammers now try to make it more difficult to spot junk Emails from their titles by using something totally misleading. Here are a few typical examples:

Re Reservation #12398965

Re your recent order

Re I have still not had a reply

Re Your In Box has reached its size limit

Re Here is the information you requested

Re Returned mail – user unknown

Of course, in most cases you do not have to look too hard to see that the Email is of the junk variety. It is quite likely you will not have made a reservation, placed an order, and so on. Also, the "from" address will probably not be that of a company you deal with. However, this type of spam is more difficult to spot and probably a significant proportion of the recipients open them. In order to make these junk Emails look more authentic, some spammers use false "from" addresses that look very similar to the Email address of a large and well-known company. In some cases the actual address of the company is used.

Getting addresses

As already pointed out, most Email account suppliers have largely blocked the system of sending Emails to a large number of addresses in the hope that some of them actually exist. Therefore, spammers need large numbers of valid Email addresses in order to make their systems work. Sophisticated techniques are used to trawl the Internet for Email addresses that appear on web pages, so having your Email address on a web page more or less guarantees that you will receive plenty of spam. Usenet newsgroup postings are another source.

If you deal with respectable companies they will have agreed to respect your privacy and not pass on your

Email address to other companies. Some, provided you agree, will pass your Email address to other companies that are offering goods or services that are likely to be of interest to you. Letting them do this is a bit dubious, because it is possible that the companies they sell your address to will in turn pass it on to others. In theory this should not happen, but in practice you can find your Email address being passed along a chain of companies.

Giving your Email address to a company that is not well known to you is definitely not a good idea. Most companies will not pass your Email address on to others, but some will certainly do so. Some freebies on the Internet are probably put there specifically to gather Email addresses for spamming purposes. The way to "have your cake and eat it" is to have a main Email address that is used as your main address plus a second account that is used only for free offers and the like.

If you should find the second Email address is getting bombarded with spam it will not really matter, since it is not used for normal personal business contacts. Periodically clearing the accumulated Emails should not take long. It is easy to set up free Email accounts with the main providers, so if one dummy account becomes unusable you can always close it and open another one. You can give a company your proper Email address should you decide that they are trustworthy.

Blocking

As explained previously, many Email account providers use a certain amount of built-in blocking in an attempt to reduce the amount of spam reaching their client's Inboxes. Checking the title field or other parts of an Email for certain words or phrases is known as content blocking or content filtering. It is not very effective in practice. As already pointed out, many spammers use deliberate misspellings to circumvent this type of filtering. The other problem is that taking this type of filtering to the point where it is effective at filtering spam is likely to result in many legitimate Emails being blocked as well.

The main weapon against spam at present is address blocking, where the Email companies have lists of addresses that are used as the sources for junk Emails. Any Email traffic from these addresses is blocked. This method can block many Emails, but it will never be totally effective because those compiling the lists of banned addresses are inevitably one step behind those sending out the spam. An address must be used to send out at least one batch of spam before it can be detected and added to the blacklist. The spammer can then switch to a new address. Some spam is blocked and the blacklists make life difficult for those sending junk Emails, but this method can never block all spam.

Some Email companies provide their clients with customisable blocking facilities. This type of thing is likely to have limited effectiveness against spam in general, but it can be totally effective in combating the same old junk mails turning up in your Inbox time and time again. The obvious form of filtering to use with persistent junk mail is to simply filter its source address. As pointed out previously, spam often originates from dummy addresses that are changed frequently, so blocking an address might not block further occurrences of the same Email. This system can be very effective in cases where a company keeps sending you details of their latest special offers (or whatever) despite your repeated requests for them to desist. They will presumably send the Emails from their legitimate address, and blocking this address will therefore stop the junk Emails from finding their way into your Inbox.

Some Email companies permit a degree of content filtering. This is again something that can be useful for combating persistent spam, particularly if it has the same or largely the same wording. For example, a while ago I had problems with a company selling off the shelf university degrees that seemed to Email me at least twice per day and three times per day at weekends. The title field of the email always contained the word "diploma", so I was able to halt the flow of Emails from this source by setting up the Email system to filter any Email with this word in the title. Obviously some persistent spam will not be this obliging, but it is a useful system in those cases where it can be applied with at least partial success.

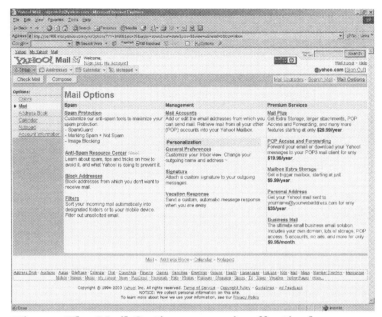

Fig.3.1 The Mail Options page is effectively a large menu

Setting up

The spam and general facilities on offer vary from one Email system to another. With the popular Yahoo! Email service the Mail Options link takes you to a page where various facilities can be accessed (Figure 3.1). The Spam Protection link is the obvious starting point, and this takes you to the page shown in Figure 3.2. Yahoo! has a facility that it calls Spam Guard, and its basic function is to look for what are likely to be junk Emails. Any that the system finds are placed in the Bulk folder. They will be deleted after 30 days unless you move them or delete them first. The first

3   Spam, spam, spam

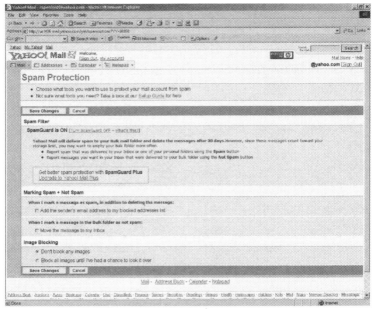

Fig.3.2 The Spam Protection page of Yahoo!

page enables the Spam Guard function to be switched
on or off.

The checkboxes near the bottom of the page provide
a couple of options. One of these automatically adds
the sender's Email address to your blocked list when
you mark an Email as spam. As pointed out
previously, spammers tend to change the sender's
address quite often, so using this facility might just
produce a large but ineffective list of blocked
addresses. Using it will not do any harm though. The
second option automatically moves a message to your
Inbox if you mark it as not being spam. This saves
you the bother of having to move it manually, so it is
probably as well to tick this checkbox.

The radio buttons at the bottom of the page provide the option of displaying graphics in bulk Emails or suppressing them. The graphics content is not necessarily in the Email itself, but instead the Email carries the address of a web page that contains the image files. When you open the Email, the web page is opened and the graphics content is displayed within the Email. This assumes that your Email client is one that can handle HTML, as most can these days. With a text-only service the Emails will not appear on the page, and the web address for the page that contains them will be displayed instead.

Obviously the Yahoo! Email service can handle HTML and graphics, and normally any graphics will be displayed when you open an Email. Although this might not seem to be of any importance, it can potentially alert the sender to the fact that you have opened the Email, and that your Email address is an active one. This is likely to result in an increase in the amount of spam directed to your Email address. It is therefore advisable to switch off the display of any graphic content. Note that this option only affects mail in the Bulk folder and that Emails in any other folders will still have the graphics displayed in the normal way.

In use the Spam Guard feature will not be perfect. A certain number of junk Emails will probably find their way to the Inbox, and it is then just a matter of ticking the checkbox for that piece of mail and operating the Spam button near the top of the window. Alternatively, if you have opened the Email, simply operate the

Spam button near the top of the page. Either way the Email will be sent to the Bulk folder. The opposite problem is likely to occur, with Emails you wish to receive being consigned to the Bulk folder. This is likely to happen with any Emails that are sent out as part of a mass mailing. For instance, I get financial news reports sent to me by Email, and details of all the latest special offers from several companies that sell computer bits and pieces. These Emails are also sent to thousands of other subscribers, but it is impossible for a filtering system to distinguish between legitimate bulk mailings and those from spammers.

The way around the problem is to go into an Email that has been sent to the Bulk folder by mistake, and then operate the Not Spam button near the top of the window. Any further Emails from the same source should then be directed to the Inbox. It might take a week or so to get everything working correctly, but thereafter you should find that the bulk Emails that you wish to receive are direct to the Inbox.

Checking

It is still necessary to check through the contents of the Bulk folder from time to time just in case something has been sent there by mistake. Where large amounts of junk mail are sent to this folder it might be necessary to check through it occasionally and then delete all the unwanted Emails. They will be deleted after 30 days anyway, but you could find

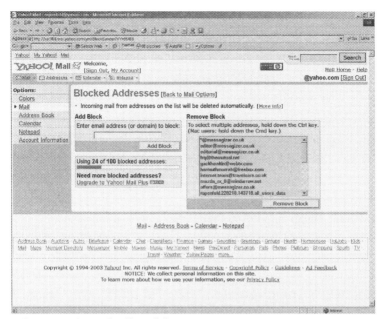

Fig.3.3 The Block Addresses page

that this is long enough for a considerable number of Emails to build up. This could result in a large percentage of your available storage space being taken up by the Bulk folder. In an extreme case it could result in the available space being used up.

An address can be added to the blocked list by going to the Mail Options page and left-clicking the Block Addresses link. This produces a page like the one shown in Figure 3.3. In order to block an address it is just a matter of typing it into the textbox and operating the Add Block button. The address will then be added to the list of blocked addresses in the right-hand section of the window. With a long address it is easier to cut and paste it into the textbox, which should also guarantee that errors are avoided. In order to remove an address from the blocked list, first select it using the normal left-clicking method and then operate the Remove Block button.

What actually happens to blocked Emails? It depends on the Email company you are using, but most operate in the same way as the Yahoo! system. Blocked Emails are not bounced back to the sender, and are actually accepted by the system. The system checks each Email to see if it needs to be blocked for some reason, and if it does, then it is deleted. Some systems place blocked Emails in the Trash folder, but it is more normal these days for block Emails to be deleted. Consequently, there is usually no way of retrieving a blocked Email so you have to be careful not to accidentally block anything important.

The Yahoo! blocking system, in common with most others, does require a complete Email address. Suppose that you are receiving nuisance Emails from a company, and that the domain name is common to all the Emails but the name ahead of the domain is different for each one. For example, these Email addresses all have the same domain name but are (supposedly) from a different person or department within the company:

fred@wxyz.co.uk

judy@wxyz.co.uk

customersupport@wxyz.co.uk

despatch@wxyz.co.uk

It is not possible to block these Emails using the full address, because it changes slightly each time a new Email is sent to you. However, if any Emails from an address ending wxyz.co.uk are blocked, then all the offending Emails will be filtered.

Careful filtering

Due care needs to be taken with this system, because it is easy to block rather more than you intended. I was once asked to assist someone who having problems with a substantial number of missing Emails. A little investigation showed that she had blocked all addresses ending "hotmail.com", not realising that Hotmail provides Email services to millions of people. This method of blocking is really only of use with companies that have their own domain name.

The Filter link on the Mail Options page gives access to a blocking style facility, but strictly speaking it does not actually block anything. What it actually does is to permit Emails to be scanned, and those that meet certain criteria are redirected to another folder. This enables, for example, Emails that are erroneously being sent to the Bulk folder to be redirected to the Inbox. It can provide a pseudo blocking action by redirecting Emails to the Trash folder where they will in due course be automatically deleted.

The first page in the filter section (Figure 3.4) shows the filters that are already in use, and it enables them to be edited or deleted. Operating the Add button

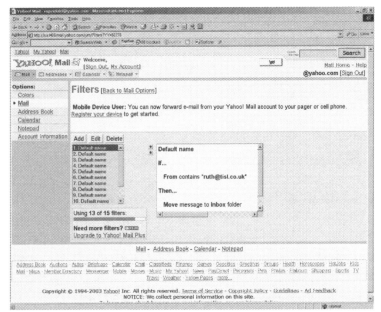

Fig.3.4 The first page shows the filters in use

switches to the page of Figure 3.5 where the settings for a new filter can be selected. The system can be set to look for a certain Email address, but it is also possible to have it search for a string of characters in other parts of each Email. In other words, it can provide content filtering if required.

Earlier I mentioned a problem with junk Emails trying to sell me "off the shelf" diplomas, and content filtering is good at dealing with this type of thing. The word "diploma" always appeared in either the subject or body fields of the Email, and usually in both. Therefore, these Emails could effectively be filtered by using the word "diploma" in both of these fields in the filter.

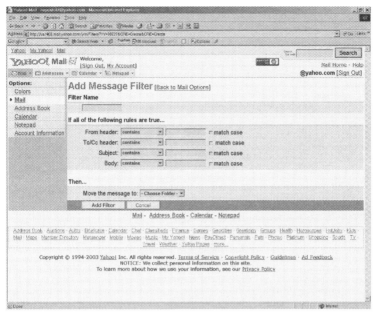

Fig.3.5 This page is used to create new filters

Trash is selected from the Move message to menu, so that the offending Emails are redirected to the Trash folder and, in due course, automatically deleted. The filter can be given a name in the textbox near the top of the window. This makes it easier to find the filter if you need to edit or erase it at a later date. Finally, operate the Add Filter button and the newly created filter will be added to the list of filters (Figure 3.6).

Of course, this type of filtering will not always be effective. As pointed out previously, some spammers now try to hide keywords from this type of filtering by using deliberate misspellings and similar tricks. In

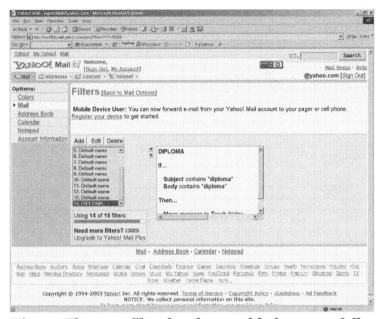

Fig.3.6 The new filter has been added successfully

this example the filtering would not detect the word "diploma if it was disguised, as in these examples:

dipl4oma6

dipploma

d-i-p-l-o-m-a

d I p l o m a

It is not really practical to add filters for all the possible variations. Nevertheless, this type of filtering can still be useful in combating a significant proportion of junk Emails.

The exact facilities on offer will obviously vary somewhat from one Email service to another, as will

Fig.3.7 The Hotmail Inbox has a Block button

the way in which those facilities are accessed. With the popular Hotmail service it is easy to block further Emails from an address. There is a Block button in the toolbar of the Inbox (Figure 3.7). Simply tick the checkbox of the offending Email and then operate the Block button. The relevant address will then be added to the list of blocked addresses.

More facilities can be accessed by activating the Options link, which produces a list of additional features (Figure 3.8). In the current context it is the Junk Email Protection link that is of interest, and this produces the page of Figure 3.9. The options on offer include a Junk Email Filter page where three degrees

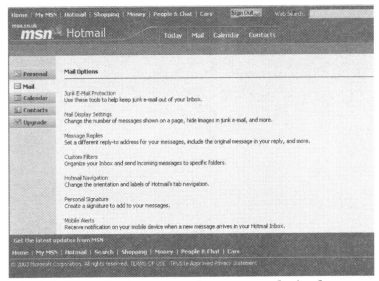

Fig.3.8 More features can be accessed via the Options link

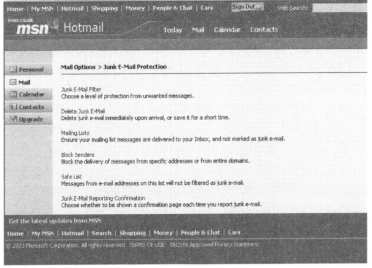

Fig.3.9 The Junk Email Protection page

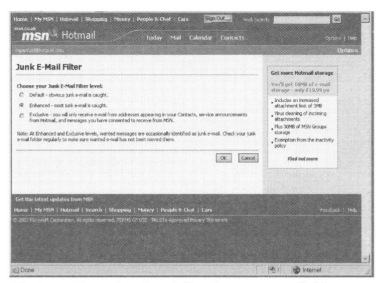

Fig.3.10 Three levels of filtering are available

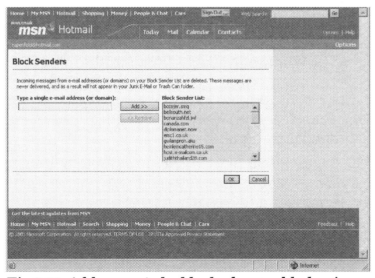

Fig.3.11 Addresses to be blocked are added using this page

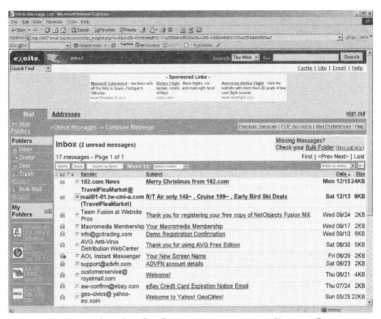

Fig.3.12 Excite includes a Report as Spam button

of protection are available (Figure 3.10). Another option enables addresses to be added to those that will be blocked (Figure 3.11). It is also possible to have junk Emails deleted immediately rather than being deposited in the Junk folder.

The Excite Email service includes a Block button as part of the Inbox (Figure 3.12), and it also has a Report as Spam button. A reporting feature of this type is quite common, and the idea is to show the programmers at the Email company the types of junk Email that are getting through the built-in filters. This should enable them to improve their systems and defeat a greater percentage of the junk Emails.

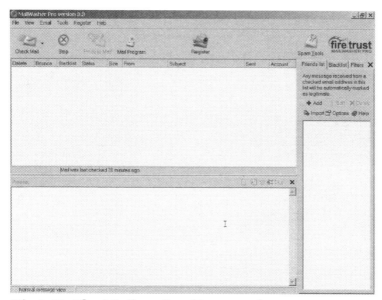

Fig.3.13 The Mailwasher Pro opening screen

Filter programs

There are several good Email programs available that can add filtering facilities not provided by your Email service, but note that these programs are not usable with all Email systems. Few seem to work with Yahoo! for example, and some do not work with Hotmail either. MailWasher Pro is an example of an add-on filter program, and this one does work with Hotmail. As far as I can ascertain, it is not usable with the Email service offered by Yahoo!

Once MailWasher Pro is installed and run, the opening screen of Figure 3.13 is obtained. In order to set up a filter the Spam Tools button is operated, and

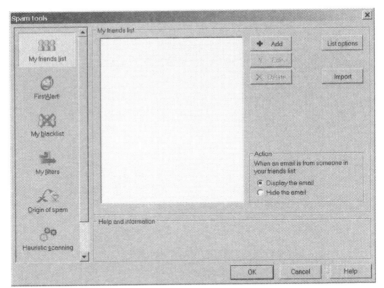

Fig.3.14 The first step in producing a new filter

this produces a window like the one shown in Figure 3.14. Here the My Filters button is pressed, and the window then changes to look like Figure 3.15. There are a couple of default filters listed here, and the Add button is operated in order to define your own filter.

This launches a new window (Figure 3.16), and the rules for the added filter are defined in the lower section of the window. There is provision for two rules by default, but the buttons permit the number of rules to be increased or reduced. The rules operate in a similar way to the Yahoo! filtering, and it is basically just a matter of giving the program a text string to search for and telling it which field or fields to search. The radio buttons give the options of the filter being activated if any one rule is met, or only if all of the

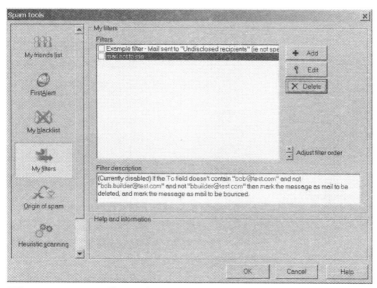

Fig.3.15 Next the Add button is operated

conditions are satisfied. The upper section of the window gives various choices about the way in which a filtered Email is treated.

The OK button is operated when the rules and other

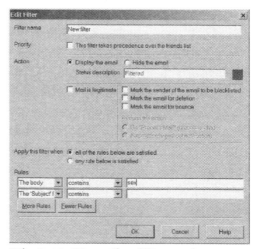

Fig.3.16 Here the filter rules are defined

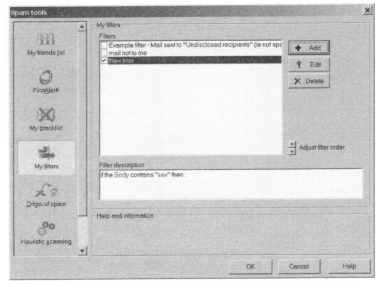

Fig.3.17 The new filter has been added to the list

options have been set up correctly, and the new filter
should then be added to the list (Figure 3.17). In this
example the filter is set up to look for the word "sex"
in the body field of the Email. I then sent two Emails
to myself, with one having the word "testing" as the
body text and the other one having the word "sex".
As can be seen from Figure 3.18, the program has
correctly filtered the second Email containing the
offending word.

Heuristic scanning

Some Email filter programs, including MailWasher
can provide heuristic scanning, and this technique is
also available in some antivirus programs. It is a

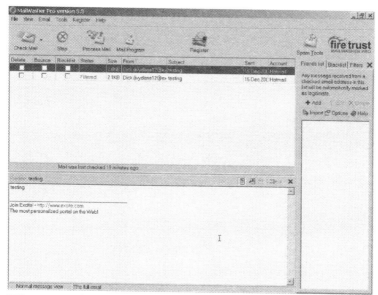

Fig.3.18 The filtering has redirected the Email

technique of looking for files that have the characteristics of viruses, or Emails that look like they are probably spam. The advantage of the heuristic approach is that it does not leave you one step behind the virus writers and the spammers.

Most viruses are actually just minor variations on those already in existence, but a normal matching process will not detect them. The new viruses are similar to existing ones, but are sufficiently different to prevent a match from being obtained. A heuristic approach is more likely to find these variations since it is looking for certain tell-tale pieces of code rather than a perfect match overall. Potentially, the heuristic approach can find new viruses that are not yet in its

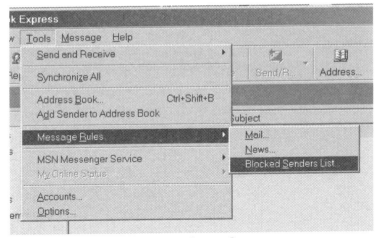

Fig.3.19 The Message Rules submenu

virus database, giving better protection. It will not find genuinely new viruses, but it will detect most of the recycled ones. The situation is similar with junk Emails, where many of them are just minor variations on previous versions in an attempt to "fool" content filtering. Again, a heuristic approach can pick up this type of thing.

Inevitably there is a drawback to this approach, and it is simply that there is a greater chance of an innocent file or Email being picked up by a system of this type. If applied too strongly to Emails you could find that many legitimate Emails are being automatically deleted of dumped into the Trash folder. MailWasher has Careful and Strong heuristic settings, and it is probably best to opt for the more cautious Careful setting.

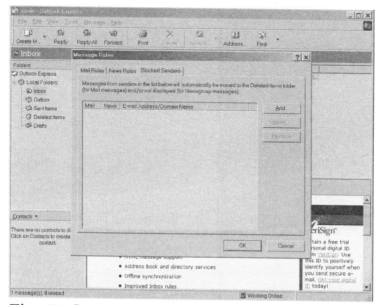

Fig.3.20 Operate the Add button to add a new address to the list

Outlook Express

Users of Outlook Express have only very limited filtering facilities built into the program. However, it is possible to block addresses. Select Message Rules from the Tools menu, followed by Blocked Senders List from the submenu that appears (Figure 3.19). A new window then appears (Figure 3.20) and the Add button is operated. A third window then appears (Figure 3.21), and the address you wish to block is entered into the textbox. The radio buttons enable new message, mail messages, or both of these to be blocked. Operate the OK button to close the window, and the newly blocked address should appear in the

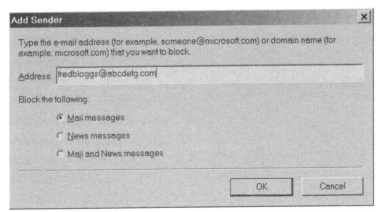

Fig.3.21 The address to be blocked is entered in the textbox

list displayed in the Message Rules window (Figure 3.22).

Unsubscribe

Sometimes junk Emails have a link that you can click in order to unsubscribe from the service. It should be possible to unsubscribe to a service in cases where you have genuinely subscribed to something in the first place. It can sometimes happen when you join some form of online club or service that you subscribe to something without realising it. Few of us take the bother to read the "fine print" when joining this type of thing. There is no risk in unsubscribing to a service that you have actually joined in the first place.

In general though, it is advisable not to activate one of these links. Many of them will not unsubscribe you

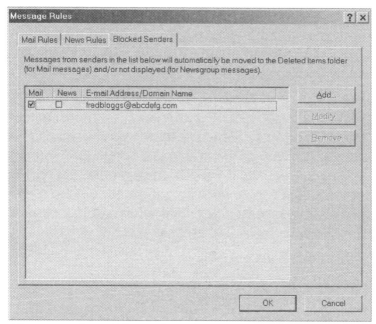

Fig.3.22 The address has been added to the list

from anything if you do activate the link. Just the opposite in fact, and by operating the link you will probably just be indicating to the spammer that he or she has found an active Email account. That account is then likely to be targeted with large amounts of spam. It is very tempting to activate these links, but it is nearly always a mistake to do so.

For the same reason it is important not to respond to spam. By doing so you are making it clear to the spammers that they have found an active account. Worse than that, you are making it clear that they have found an account that is owned by someone that is susceptible to spam. To put it bluntly, you are letting them know that they have found a mug. This more or less guarantees that you will receive ever increasing amounts of spam.

It is as well to bear in mind that the companies promoted by junk Emails are usually something less than respectable. Some are legitimate businesses of sorts, but many of the offers are bogus and you are unlikely to receive the goods if you should try buying something in response to a junk Email. Giving credit card details or other financial information to one of these companies is just plain daft.

Points to remember

Most Email services have built-in facilities that help to block much of the spam directed at your Email address. One system they use is to have a blacklist of addresses that are known to be used for sending spam. Another is to block Emails that contain certain words and phrases.

There are programs available that can be used to reduce problems with spam. These enable you to block mail from specific addresses and (or) mail that contains certain words. These facilities are built into some Email services.

Heuristic scanning filters Emails that have various characteristics associated with spam. It can work quite well if used in moderation but can filter too many legitimate Emails when used strongly.

Clicking on the unsubscribe links in spam is not a good idea. In many cases the links are "blind" and clicking on them has no effect at all. In other cases you are simply alerting the spammers to the fact that they have found an active Email account.

Do not reply to spam. The chances of getting ripped off in some way are quite high and some junk Emails are completely fraudulent. Replying to spam simply encourages the spammers to continue in their activities. If there were no replies to spam there would be no more spam.

4

Windows tuning tools

Efficient files

On the face of it, once your PC is set up correctly there should be nothing more to do, and it should go on working efficiently thereafter. In practice the situation is more difficult than this, and it is quite normal for a PC to run noticeably slower after it has been in use for a few months, or even after a few weeks of use. So why does a PC tend to slow down over a period of time? The fall-off in performance is usually due to the hard disc drive taking longer to load files into memory, but the problem is not really caused by the hardware. A PC's hardware normally works at full tilt or not at all.

The problem has more to do with the number of files on the hard disc drive. Most people add more programs and data to their PCs over a period of time. Each program that is added tends to make the Windows Registry grow ever bigger, and the newly added files tend to be spread all over the hard disc rather than grouped neatly together. Getting a PC to run efficiently therefore consists largely of removing unnecessary files and keeping the remaining files

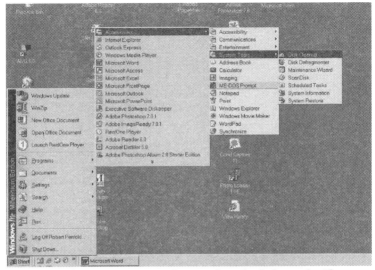

*Fig.4.1 The System Tools are buried deep in the
menu structure*

organised properly on the hard disc drive. The
Registry incidentally, is a database of settings for
Windows itself, and for any programs installed on the
PC.

Hidden tools

There are numerous utility programs available that
help to get a PC working efficiently and keep it that
way, but it would be a mistake to overlook the built-in
tools of Windows itself. It would be a mistake, but it
would also be quite easy because they are buried quite
deep in the menu structure (Figure 4.1). From the
Start menu select Programs, Accessories, System
Tools, and then the required program. A good one to
start with is Disk Cleanup. The Disk Cleanup

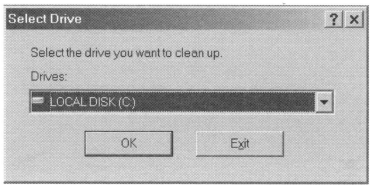

*Fig.4.2 Select the appropriate drive from the
          drop-down menu*

program used in this example is the one in Windows
ME, but essentially the same facility is available in
Windows XP.

As its name suggests, Disk Cleanup looks for
unnecessary files on the selected disc drive. The
initial window of Figure 4.2 appears, and the drop-
down menu is used to select the appropriate drive,
which will usually be the default option of drive C. The
program then scans the disc for files that it thinks
are no longer required, and a summary of its findings
is then displayed (Figure 4.3). It is not possible to
select files for deletion on an individual basis, and
there will usually be too many of them for this to be a
practical proposition. Instead, you are presented with
various file categories, and all the files in a category
can be erased by first ticking the corresponding
checkbox. The OK button is operated once all the
categories for deletion have been selected.

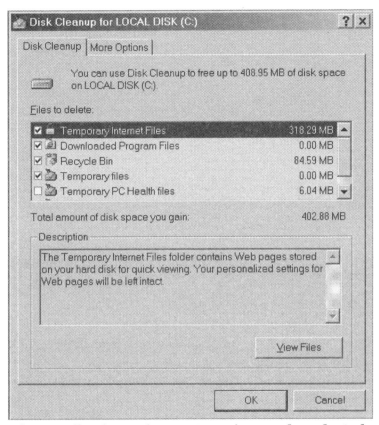

Fig.4.3 Files in various categories can be selected

The categories are slightly different depending on whether you are using Windows ME or XP, but the main ones are the same for both operating systems. The Temporary Internet Files are copies of the files downloaded when viewing Internet pages. These are stored on the hard disc in order to speed up access if you go back to the same page. Rather than downloading the page again, the copy stored on the

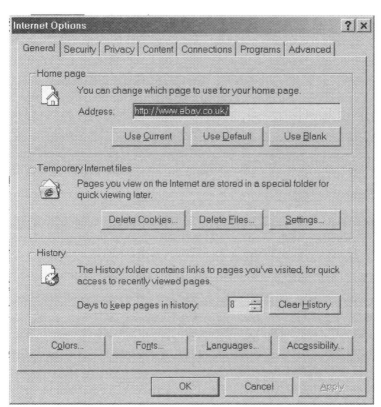

Fig.4.4 The General section of the Internet Options window

disc is used. Of course, this only works if the page has not changed since your last visit, or most of the files used in the page are the same. It is otherwise necessary for the page to be downloaded again, and a copy of the new page is stored in the cache on the hard disc. This leads to a gradual build-up of files on the hard disc, especially if you do a lot of research on the Internet and visit dozens of sites.

The files are not stored indefinitely on the disc, and Windows automatically deletes the oldest files once a certain a certain amount of disc space has been used. It is easy to alter the maximum amount of disc space that is used for this temporary storage. Start by going into Internet Explorer and then select Internet Options from the Tools menu. This produces a window like the one in Figure 4.4. The General tab will probably be selected by default, but if necessary select it manually.

The temporary Internet files can be erased by operating the Delete Files button near the middle of the window. To alter the maximum amount of space used for these temporary files, operate the Settings button just to the right of the Delete Files button, which will produce the window of Figure 4.5. Use the slider control to set the required cache size and then operate the OK button. This makes the change take effect and moves things back to the Internet Properties window. Operate the OK button in this window in order to close it.

Is it worth reducing the size of the cache for temporary Internet files and deleting its contents from time to time? This really depends on the setup you are using and the way in which it is used. With a broadband Internet connection the caching system does not necessarily bring great benefits, since most pages will probably download quite fast. It will only be of real help when downloading pages that contain large files or accessing sites that are stored on slow or very busy servers. When using an ordinary dialup

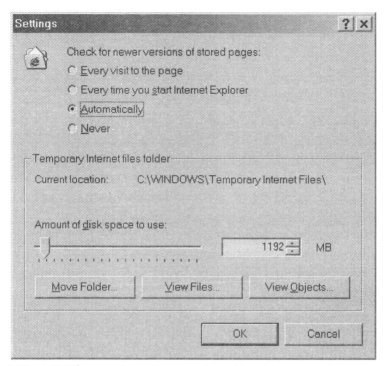

Fig.4.5 The cache size can be altered using the slider control

connection the benefits of caching are likely to be much greater. Of course, caching is ineffective with any system if you do not keep going back to the same old web pages, or you do but there are substantial changes each time you visit them.

In practice, and regardless of the theory, the caching system does seem to be ineffective when you have a cache that occupies hundreds of megabytes or more of hard disc space, and what is likely to be tens of thousands of files. If you use Windows Explorer to go into the Temporary Internet folder it could well take the program half a minute to produce a list of all the files, and the number of files could well be in excess of 50 thousand. This gives a hint as to why the caching system can become inefficient.

A large cache of temporary Internet files can be particularly inefficient if there is a lack of vacant hard disc space. Allocating a large amount of space for temporary Internet storage could greatly reduce the amount of disc space left for other forms of temporary storage, causing a significant reduction in the overall performance of the PC. If spare hard disc space is strictly limited it is definitely a good idea to reduce the amount of space allocated to storing temporary Internet files.

Having erased the temporary Internet cache it is likely that Internet access will be a bit slower initially when using your favourite sites. This will be especially noticeable with slow sites or when using a dialup connection. However, the cached files will be reinstated after visiting each of these sites for the first time, so any slowdown will be only temporary.

Temporary files

Returning to the categories of files listed by the Disk Cleanup program, the Temporary Files category contains files that that have been placed in a "TEMP" folder by applications programs. Many applications generate temporary files that are normally erased when the program is closed. However, some of these files get left behind, possibly due to a program shutting down abnormally. Some programs are not designed quite as well as they might be and habitually leave temporary files on the hard disc drive. The files included in this category are temporary types that are more than one week old, and it should be safe to delete them. Doing so is unlikely to free much hard disc space though.

Recycle Bin

As most Windows users are no doubt aware, when you delete files they are not deleted immediately but are instead placed in the Recycle Bin. The Recycle Bin is just a folder on drive C, but it is one that is normally accessed via the icon on the Windows desktop. Special facilities are provided when the Recycle Bin is accessed, including the ability to restore any files it contains to their previous place on the hard disc. Of course, Windows does not continue storing deleted files indefinitely. There is an upper limit to the size of the Recycle Bin, and eventually old deleted files will be completely removed in order to make space for newer ones.

The default size for the Recycle Bin is quite large, so a substantial number of files can be amassed over a period of time. It can be altered by right-clicking on the Recycle Bin icon and selecting Properties from the pop-up menu. This produces the window of Figure 4.6, and the maximum size of the Recycle Bin can then be set via the slider control. Note that the percentage

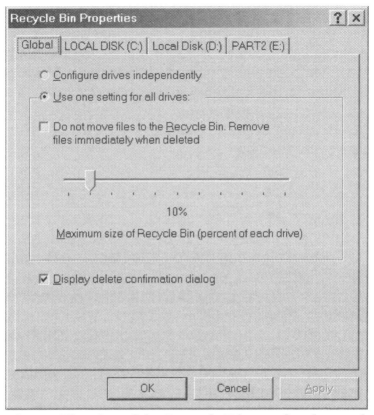

Fig.4.6 The size of the Recycle Bin can be changed

set here is the percentage of each drive's full capacity that will be used for storing deleted files. It does not represent the percentage of free disc space that will be used for this purpose. Accordingly, it is best to settle for a small figure here if a disc's capacity has been largely used up.

By default, the same percentage is used for all the discs. If preferred though, the "Configure drives independently" radio button can be operated. The size of the Recycle Bin can then be set individually for each drive. Simply operate the tab for the drive you wish to alter and then use the slider control to set the required maximum size.

It is not necessary to utilise the Recycle Bin at all. It can be switched off by ticking the checkbox just above the slider control, and deleted files will then be fully erased at once. It is not really necessary to use this option, since the Recycle Bin can be circumvented by selecting the files to be deleted, holding down the Shift key, and then operating the Del key or selecting the Delete option from the appropriate menu. The usual warning message will still appear so that you have a chance to change your mind before the files are deleted. This message can be suppressed by ticking the checkbox near the bottom of the Recycle Bin Properties window.

When fully deleting files, whether via the Disk Cleanup program or by other means, bear in mind that Windows offers no way of retrieving files once they have been fully deleted. It is often possible to retrieve deleted files using an undelete utility, but there is no guarantee that this will be possible. It will certainly not be possible to retrieve a file once the disc space it occupied has been overwritten by another file. Even with a partially overwritten file there is little prospect of retrieving anything worthwhile.

The rest

The other categories in the Disk Cleanup program tend to be those concerned with things such as diagnostics. These files are not necessarily of any use, but there will probably be little point in deleting them. The number of files and the disc space that they occupy will both be quite small, if there are actually any files at all.

Defragmenters

Many users tend to assume that files are automatically stored on the hard disc on the basis of one continuous section of disc per file. Unfortunately, it does not necessarily operate in this fashion. When Windows is first installed on a PC it is likely that files will be added in this fashion. The applications programs are then installed, and things will probably continue in an organised fashion with files stored on the disc as single clumps of data. Even if things have progressed well thus far, matters soon take a turn for the worse when the user starts deleting files, adding new files or programs, deleting more files, and so on.

Gaps are produced in the continuous block of data when files are deleted. Windows utilises the gaps when new data is added, but it will use them even if each one is not large enough to take a complete file. If necessary, it will use dozens of these small vacant areas to accommodate a large file. This can result in a large file being spread across the disc in numerous tiny packets of data, which makes reading the file a relatively slow and inefficient business. The computer

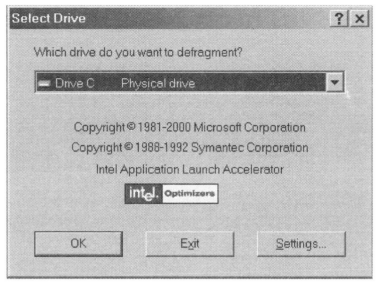

Fig.4.7 The Windows ME defragmenter

can seriously slow down when a substantial number of files get fragmented in this way.

There are programs called defragmenters that reorganise the files on a disc drive so that, as far as reasonably possible, large files are not fragmented. A program of this type is available in the System Tools submenu as the Disk Defragmenter. This utility has something of a chequered past, and in older versions of Windows it gave odd results with some disc drives. At some point in the proceedings the estimated time to completion would start to rise and usually kept rising with the process never finishing. Provided you are using a reasonably modern version of Windows there should be no problem of this type and the Disk Defragmenter program should work well.

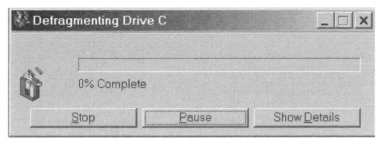

*Fig.4.8 A bargraph show how things are
        progressing*

On launching the Windows ME version of the program
a window like the one shown in Figure 4.7 is produced.
The pop-down menu is used to select the disc drive
that will be processed and then the OK button is
operated. This produces a small window like the one
shown in Figure 4.8. This indicates how far the disc
processing has progressed, and it will eventually
report that the process has been completed. With a
large disc that is badly fragmented it can take several
hours for the process to be completed.

The defragmenter program supplied as part of
Windows XP is a more sophisticated affair than the
Windows ME version. Launching the program
produces a large window like the one that appears in
Figure 4.9. The drives that can be defragmented are
listed in the main section of the window, and in this
case there are two drives that are actually partitions
on the same physical drive. These are treated as two
separate entities by the operating system, and they
are therefore processed in that way by defragmenter
programs.

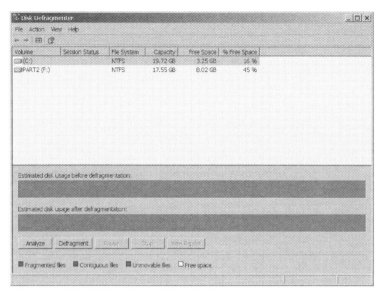

Fig.4.9 The Windows XP defragmenter program

While it is possible to jump straight in and start processing the selected drive, this version of Disk Defragmenter offers the alternative of first analysing the drive to determine how badly (or otherwise) it is fragmented. There is little point in defragmenting a disc that is performing well. To analyse the disc either operate the Analyze button near the bottom left-hand corner of the window or select Analyze from the Actions menu. In this example the analysis produced the result shown in Figure 4.10.

A small window pops up and indicates whether it is worthwhile defragmenting the disc. In this example it indicates that the disc a severely fragmented and that the defragmenter program should be set to work.

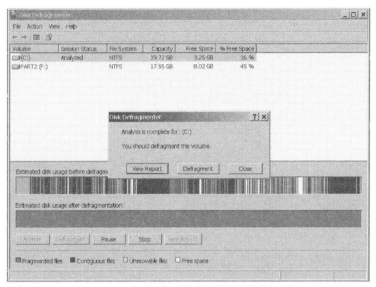

Fig.4.10 The results of analysing drive C

There is a bar across the window that shows fragmented files in red and the contiguous files in blue (mid and dark grey respectively in Figure 4.10). Although a lot of contiguous files are in evidence, together with unused disc space and unmovable system files, there is a significant amount of red scattered along the bar. More information about the state of the disc can be obtained by operating the View Report button in the pop-up window. This produces some general information about the hard disc in addition to more specific information about individual files (Figure 4.11).

In order to go ahead with the processing operate the Defragment button in the pop-up window. You can

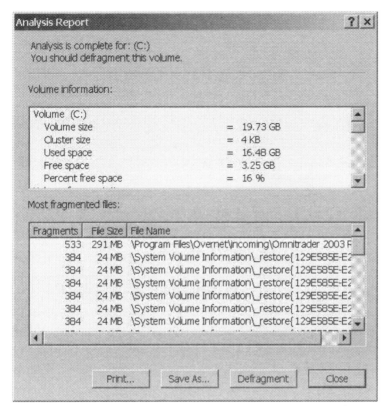

Fig.4.11 Some general information about the disc can be provided

jump straight to this stage without analysing the disc first by operating the Defragment button in the main window. Either way, the lower part of the window will show two bars, with the upper one showing the initial state of the disc. The lower bar shows how the processing is progressing.

Eventually the process will be completed and a window like the one in Figure 4.12 will appear. This

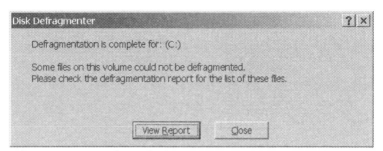

*Fig.4.12   Complete defragmentation is not always
            possible*

will often report that, as in this case, it was not
possible to fully defragment the disc. However, there
should be a substantial improvement. Regular use
of Disk Defragmenter should gradually get the disc
to the point where it is fully defragmented, or nearly
so. The two bars in the lower section of the main
window shows the "before" and "after" states of the
disc (Figure 4.13).

Scandisk

Scandisk is another of the Windows System Tools, and
it is familiar to most Windows users. If Windows is
improperly shut down it is virtually certain that
Scandisk will be run automatically when the PC is
rebooted. Although it is mainly run by Windows itself,
it is possible for the user to run it at any time. Due to
its tendency to pop up unannounced, Scandisk tends
to be regarded as a nuisance by many users, but it is
a very useful piece of software.

The purpose of Scandisk is to examine the file and
folder structure of a disc in a search for errors. It is

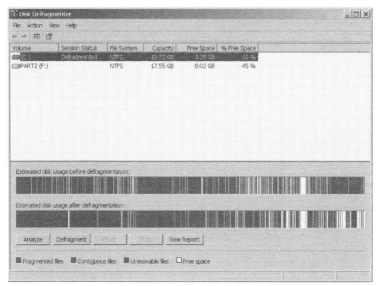

Fig.4.13 The "before" and "after" diagrams

worthwhile using this program when a PC seems to take a long time to complete disc accesses, has a tendency to crash, takes much longer than normal to boot into Windows, or shows a reluctance to start up or close down properly. Note that Scandisk is not available under Windows XP, but it is available in Windows ME and its predecessors.

The Scandisk utility offers two modes of operation. These are Standard and Thorough modes, and you operate the radio buttons to select the one you require (Figure 4.14). The Standard check looks for irregularities in the file and folder structure. This includes simple things like filenames that do not adhere to the rules, and more serious problems such as one sector of the disc being assigned to two or more

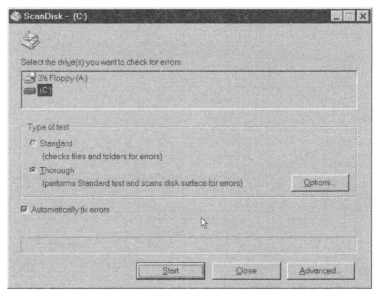

Fig.4.14   There are Standard and Thorough modes

files. Program crashes can leave problems of these types, so it is not a bad idea to run Scandisk if a program comes to an unscheduled finish. If you tick the appropriate checkbox Scandisk will try to repair any errors that it finds.

Initially I would recommend using the Standard mode with the checkbox ticked. This test should be relatively fast, taking no more than a few minutes. If the program discovers any problems it will report them via onscreen messages, and at the end it also gives a brief summary of its findings (Figure 4.15). Unfortunately, if Scandisk does find some errors and fixes them, this does not necessarily mean that Windows will then work perfectly. The problems will

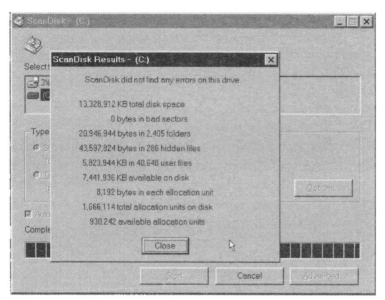

Fig.4.15 A summary of the results is provided

be fixed in the sense that filenames will adhere to the rules, linked files will be unlinked so that each sector of the disc is assigned to only one file, and so on. Any damaged files may not be fully restored using Scandisk. If one file partly overwrites another file there is no way that a utility program such as Scandisk can restore the overwritten part of the file. Unless you have a backup copy the damaged file will be lost permanently. However, Scandisk should at least restore order to the disc if things have gone wrong, improving the chances of getting things running smoothly again.

The Thorough mode performs the same tests as the Standard mode, but it additionally carries out a

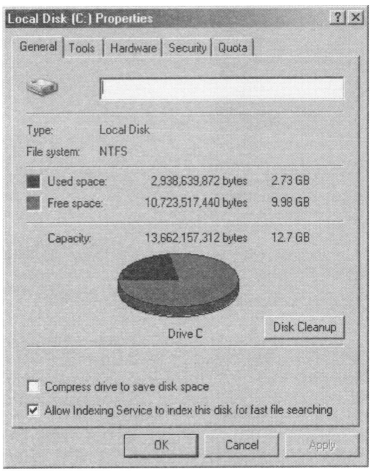

Fig.4.16 The Properties window for drive C

surface scan of the disc. In other words, it checks
that there are no weak spots on the disc that are
causing data to become corrupted. It is certainly
worth using the Thorough mode if you suspect that
the disc itself may be causing problems. Note though,

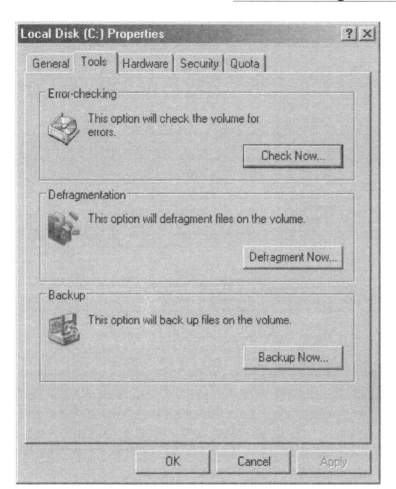

Fig.4.17 The Properties window Tools section

that a thorough check of this type on a large hard disc
drive will take quite a long time. It will probably take
several hours rather than a few minutes for the test
to be completed.

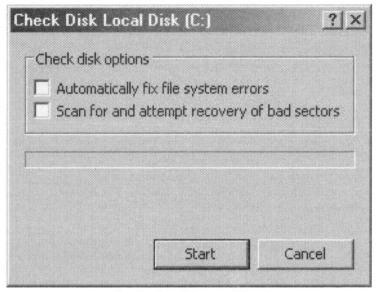

Fig.4.18 Leave both checkboxes blank

Check Disk

The Windows XP equivalent of Scandisk is the Check Disk program. This is supplied in two versions, which are a graphical user interface program and a command line utility (Chkdsk.exe). For most purposes the graphical user interface program will suffice, and this is easily accessed. In My Computer or Windows Explorer, right-click the entry for the drive you wish to check and then choose Properties from the popup menu. This produces a window like the one of Figure 4.16, which gives some basic information about the drive.

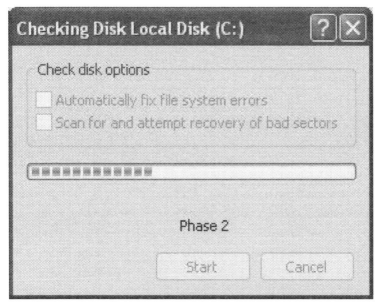

Fig.4.19 A bargraph shows how things are going

Operate the Tools tab to switch to a window like the one in Figure 4.17, which includes an error checking facility. Left-clicking the Check Now button produces the small window of Figure 4.18, where two options are available via the checkboxes. Initially it is probably best to leave both checkboxes blank, and to go ahead with the checking process by operating the Start button. The program will then check the disc for errors, showing its progress in the lower section of the window (Figure 4.19). Once the process has been completed, the program will either report that there were no errors or give a list of the problems that were detected.

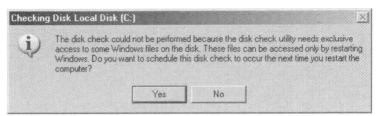

Fig.4.20 It is not possible to check a disc that is in use

If faults were detected it is advisable to run the program again, but using one or both of the options provided by the checkboxes. One option sets the program to automatically fix any errors that are detected. This is the quicker of the two options. The second option results in the program going through a very thorough checking process. It will try to recover located bad sectors on the disc and recover any data contained by those sectors. Using this option helps to minimise the damage caused by disc errors, but with large drives it can many hours for the task to be completed. Once underway there is no way out of the program other than switching off the computer, which has the potential to increase the number of disc errors and is definitely not a good idea.

The program is unable to fix errors in a disc that is currently in use, which means that it can not check the boot drive while Windows is running. Trying to check a disc that is currently in use produces the error message of Figure 4.20. To go ahead with the checking and fixing process, operate the Yes button and restart the computer. The checking program will be launched during the boot process, before the boot drive is left

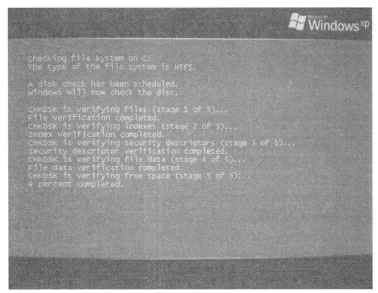

Fig.4.21 Checking takes place during boot-up

with any open files. The screen will show how things are progressing (Figure 4.21), and the boot process will continue once the disc checker has completed its task.

Users of Windows 9x operating systems soon become used to Scandisk running automatically during the boot routine if the computer has not been shut down properly. Check Disk is likely to run automatically at boot-up if a system having a FAT32 boot disc is shut down abnormally, but it is unlikely to run automatically in systems that have a NTFS boot disc. This is because the NTFS system is better able to recover from abnormal disc activity, making it unnecessary to run Check Disc at the slightest excuse. There is probably no point in running Check Disc manually if the computer was not shut down properly, because it is unlikely that any disc writing errors would have been produced.

Processes

Background processes are important to modern computing and provide a number of useful tasks. For example, an antivirus program running in the background can protect your PC from infection, dealing with viruses and computer pests before they have a chance to do any harm. The problem with background processes is that too many of them running at once can hog a PC's resources. The processing time and memory used by each process will probably be quite small, but with ten processing running the overall drain on the PC's resources could be considerable. In fact having a large number of these processes running simultaneously would almost certainly slow down even the most potent of PCs.

A big problem with background processes is that many of them are installed automatically when applications programs are loaded onto a PC. The installation program might explain that a background process will be installed, and there is sometimes an option to omit it from the installation. In practice few users pay any attention to these options when installing new software. If you simply opt for "default" or "typical" installations it is likely that your PC will soon be running some additional background tasks.

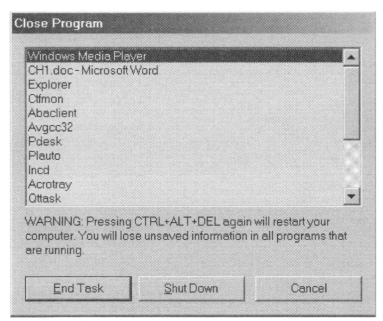

Fig.4.22   The current processes and programs are listed

The exact purpose of many background processes is something less than obvious, but many of them are intended to make things happen faster when using a certain facility of an application program. This is fine if you make frequent use of the program and facility in question, but the overhead on the PC's performance is unlikely to be justified in the case of an infrequently used feature. Where possible, it makes sense to suppress background tasks that do not "earn their keep".

Under Windows 98/ME it is possible to obtain a list of all the programs and processes that are running by operating and holding down the Control, Alt, and

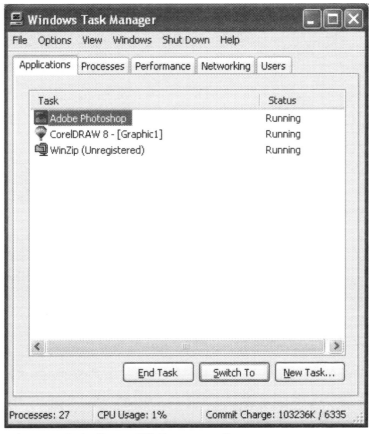

Fig.4.23 Windows XP has a task manager

Delete keys. This produces the Close Program window (Figure 4.22), and provided there are no applications programs running at the time, all the entries will be for background processes. Do not be surprised if there are more than a dozen entries in the list. Some of these will be processes used by the

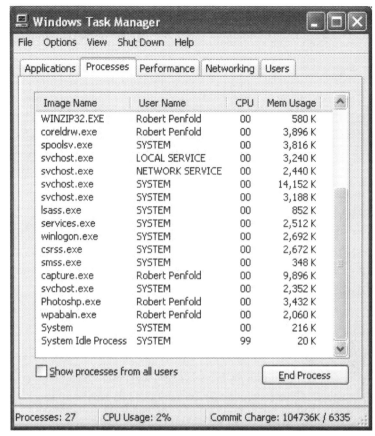

Fig.4.24 The processes are listed separately

operating system rather than user processes such as antivirus programs.

The same key combination can be used under Windows XP to launch the Windows Task Manager, but it will be necessary to operate the Task Manager button in the first window that appears. Holding down the Control, Shift, and Escape keys will launch Task Manager immediately. Either way a window like the one in Figure 4.23 will appear.

Task Manager lists applications programs and processes separately, and by default it will probably list any applications programs you are running at the time. Operate the Processes tab to produce a list of the background processes that are running (Figure 4.24). The list will be pretty long, but a substantial proportion of the processes will be part of Windows. For example, all the entries marked "SYSTEM" in the User Name column are part of the operating system. The ones that have the name of the current user in this column are the background tasks that are probably optional.

Identification

A process can be switched off by selecting its entry and then operating the End Task or End Process button. However, this is a rather clumsy way of handling things since it would be necessary to use this method each time the PC was booted. Ideally, the unnecessary processes should be prevented from automatically starting at switch-on. First there is the minor matter of identifying each process and determining its function. In some cases the names listed by Task Manager will make it clear which programs the processes are associated with. Many of the names used are decidedly cryptic though.

The easy way to identify processes is to use the name of the process in an Internet search engine such as

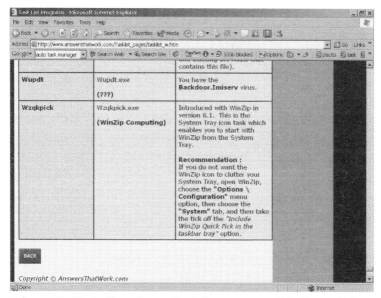

| Wupdt | Wupdt.exe

(???) | You have the **Backdoor.Imiserv** virus. |
| Wzqkpick | Wzqkpick.exe

(WinZip Computing) | Introduced with WinZip in version 8.1. This is the System Tray icon task which enables you to start with WinZip from the System Tray.

Recommendation :
If you do not want the WinZip icon to clutter your System Tray, open WinZip, choose the **"Options \ Configuration"** menu option, then choose the **"System"** tab, and then take the tick off the *"Include WinZip Quick Pick in the taskbar tray"* option. |

BACK

Copyright © AnswersThatWork.com

Fig.4.25 Details of wzqkpick are provided, and it turns out to be part of Winzip

Google, together with something like "Task Manager" or "background processes". There are a number of sites that give details of all the background processes that they have managed to identify, and the search will probably lead you to one of these.

There are several sites that specialise in this type of information, or that have a section that deals specifically with this type of thing. One of the best known is www.answersthatwork.com (Figure 4.25). While working on this book I found a process called wzqkpick, which was not one that I had noticed before. Using the processes library of this site I soon discovered that it was part of the popular WinZip file compression and decompression program. It was

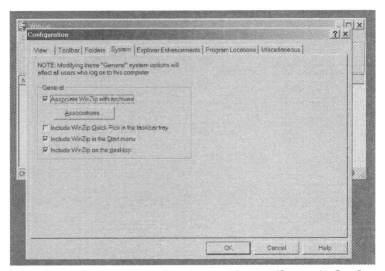

Fig.4.26 The wzqkpick process is easily switched off

part of the new version of the program that I had just installed, and had not been included with the old version installed previously. It had a matching button on the System Tray, and a check of these buttons will often help to identify background processes.

There are three basic approaches to removing a process that is not really of any great use to you. The most simple of these is to uninstall the software associated with the process. In the case of wzqkpick for example, uninstalling the WinZip program would also remove this process. The obvious problem with this method is that you will often need the program even though you have no requirement for the offending process. In this case I was certainly not prepared to uninstall WinZip.

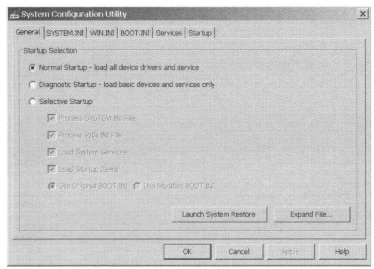

Fig.4.27 The System Configuration Utility

Method number two is to look through the options available within the program to see if there is any way of switching off the unwanted process. Most programs have a menu entry such as Options or Configuration somewhere in the menu structure. In the case of WinZip it was just a matter of selecting the Configuration option and then operating the System tab. This produced the window of Figure 4.26, and removing the tick from the appropriate checkbox suppressed the wzqkpick process. Note that this type of change does not usually take effect until the PC is rebooted.

System Configuration Utility

The third approach is to use the built-in facility of Windows called the System Configuration Facility.

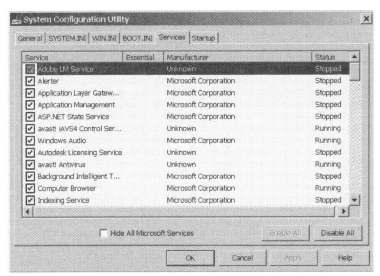

Fig.4.28 Processes listed in the Services section

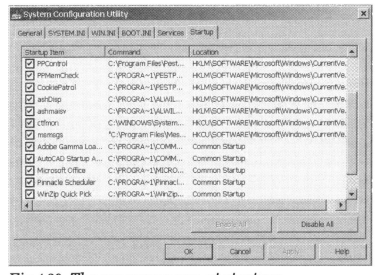

Fig.4.29 The programs run at start-up

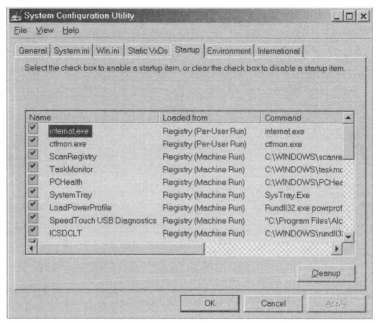

Fig.4.30 The Windows Me version of the utility is broadly similar

This can be launched by selecting Run from the Start menu and typing "msconfig" into the textbox of the small window that appears. Operating the OK button will then produce a window similar to the one shown in Figure 4.27. The General section will probably be shown by default, but other sections such as Services (Figure 4.28) and Startup (Figure 4.29) are the ones of interest in the current context. Figures 4.27 to 4.29 show the Windows XP version of the System Configuration Utility. The Windows ME version (Figure 4.30) is slightly different, but it provides essentially the same facilities.

These list various processes, and there is a checkbox for each one. Deleting the tick in its checkbox will result in the corresponding process being suppressed each time the PC is booted. Having made the required changes, operate the Apply and Close buttons, and then opt to restart the computer when prompted. The computer will then reboot and the unwanted processes will be suppressed. This method of deactivating processes is really only intended for diagnostic purposes. It provides an easy means of switching off processes but it is also easy to reinstate them again if they prove to be more important than you originally thought. Where a process does turn out to be unnecessary, it is better to reinstate it in the System Configuration Utility and then find another way of removing the process.

The System Configuration Utility could be used as a means of permanently suppressing processes where no alternative can be found, but it should only be used in this way if a desperation measure is needed. Do not simply locate and delete the program file for a process in order to prevent it from running at start-up. This will actually have the desired effect, but it will also produce an error message when Windows tries to run the program and finds the executable file missing. With processes that are simply not useful rather than actually causing a nuisance, it is probably better to leave them running if no easy method of removal can be found. This is certainly better than messing up the system by using a partially successful method of removal.

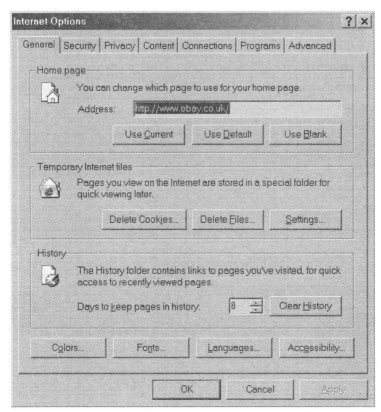

*Fig.4.31   Operating the Delete Cookies button will
remove all cookies from the PC*

Cookies

The subject of cookies was covered in chapter 1, so it
will not be covered in great detail again here. As
pointed out previously, a cookie is just a text file that
is deposited on the hard disc drive of your PC when
certain web sites are visited. Large numbers of them
can soon accumulate on the hard disc drive. Since a

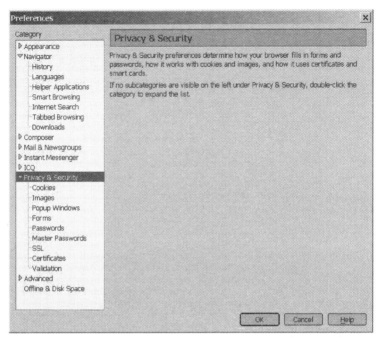

Fig.4.32 Controlling privacy and security settings in Netscape

cookie is just a small text file it should be completely innocuous, but having tousands of them build up on the hard disc is still undesirable. Consequently, it is advisable to use the built-in facilities of Windows to clear them all from time to time.

By clearing all the cookies it is likely that the automatic facilities of some web sites will be temporarily lost. For example, in chapter 1 it was pointed out that the Amazon.co.uk web site automatically recognises me each time I visit the site. Clearing all the cookies results in this type of facility being lost until you logon again. A new cookie is then

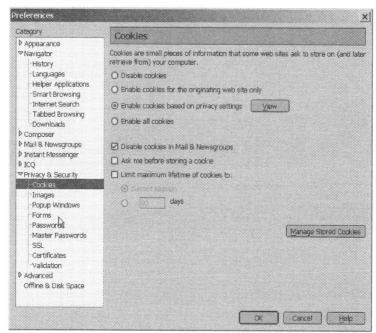

Fig.4.33 The treatment of cookies is controlled by way of this window

deposited on your PC and the site will recognise you on subsequent visits. To be more precise, the site will recognise your PC on subsequent visits. In order to delete all the cookies, start by running Internet Explorer. Select Internet Options from the Tools menu and then operate the Delete Cookies button in the new window that opens (Figure 4.31).

Netscape

Internet Explorer is by far the most popular browser, but there are others in use, and they have different means of controlling privacy and security settings.

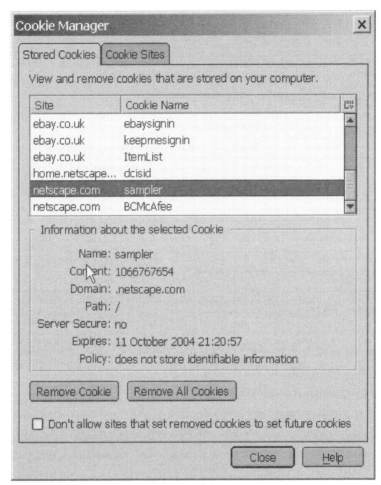

Fig.4.34 The Netscape Cookie Manager

Netscape Navigator is the main rival to Internet Explorer, and it has some useful settings that govern privacy and security, including facilities for handling cookies. These can be accessed by first selecting

Preferences from the Edit menu, which launches the Preferences window. Then double-click the Privacy & Security entry in the list down the left-hand side of the window. This will expand the entry to show its constituent parts (Figure 4.32). You can then double-click one of these parts to bring up the appropriate options in the right-hand section of the Preferences window (Figure 4.33). It is possible to control the way in which cookies and pop-ups are handled, whether or not passwords should be remembered, and so on.

Further facilities for handling cookies are available from the Cookie Manager which is accessed via the Tools menu. In addition to the ability to accept cookies, there is a manager facility for stored cookies (Figure 4.34). This shows a list of cookies, together with the site that stored each one. This makes it easy to find and remove unwanted cookies, and there is also a button that enables all the stored cookies to be removed.

Keep it simple

A PC that has a fancy Desktop and other clever features might look quite impressive, but do the clever features actually make it any better to use? These features almost invariably have an overhead in terms of reduced overall performance, so they are something to give a "wide berth" if you are seeking the greatest possible speed from you PC. In fact, the simpler the setup the faster a PC is likely to run. Even having something other than a plain background for the Windows Desktop will use memory and thus give a slight reduction in performance.

As standard, Windows XP uses the familiar field and sky background image, but it is easy to change this to a plain background. First select Control Panel from the Start menu, which will launch the Windows Control Panel. Double-click the Display icon and then select the Desktop page in the new window that appears (Figure 4.35). Select None from the list of Desktop designs in the bottom left-hand section of the window, and then select Apply and OK to make the changes take effect. This will give the traditional plain blue background to the Windows Desktop. Also avoid using screensavers if you wish to minimise unnecessary use of the PC's resources.

Swap file

If Windows starts to run short of real memory, or "physical" memory as it is often termed, it uses space on the hard disc drive as so-called virtual memory. Virtual memory is inevitably much slower than real memory, so it is advisable to have plenty of the real thing installed in a PC if high performance is required. It is not essential for the user to become involved with virtual memory, since Windows will handle the allocation of disc space for this task.

However, the performance of virtual memory can be improved by having a separate swap file. This means having a separate partition that is only used for the swap file. This partition can be part of the main (boot)

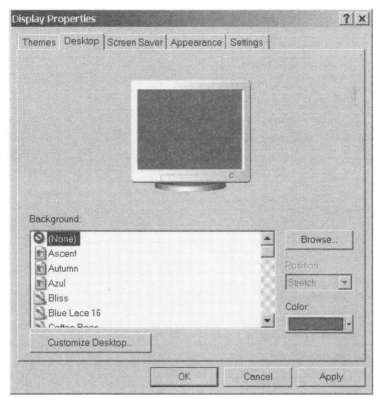

Fig.4.35 A plain desktop helps to conserve memory

drive or it can be provided by a second hard disc drive. There seems to be some disagreement about the effectiveness of having a separate swap file provided by a partition on the main hard disc. With many PCs having hard disc capacities that are well in excess of anything the user is likely to use, there is little to be lost by setting a few gigabytes aside as a separate partition for use as a swap file.

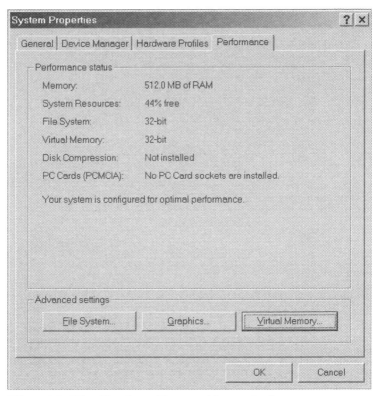

Fig.4.36 The System Properties window

Although hard disc drives are relatively cheap these days, installing one for swap file use will still cost a significant amount of money. It would probably be worthwhile for a PC that is used for memory intensive applications such as video or graphics editing, but is otherwise unlikely to be worth the money and effort involved.

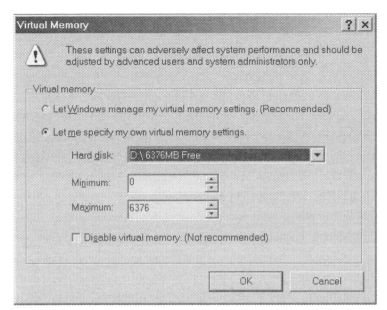

Fig.4.37 Here the drive for the swap file can be specified

Having created a new partition for a swap file, installed a second hard disc drive, or whatever, it is easy to use it for a separate swap file. Launch the Windows Control Panel and then double-click the System icon. This produces the System Properties window, where the Performance tab is operated. This gives a window like the one shown in Figure 4.36. Next, operate the Virtual Memory button to launch the Virtual Memory window (Figure 4.37). Here you have to operate the lower radio button so that you can specify your own settings. Then the appropriate drive or partition is selected from the pop-down Hard Disk menu.

A maximum size for the swap file can be specified, but the idea is to have the disc or partition used for nothing other than the swap file. Accordingly, there would seem to be no point in using anything other than the default setting, which will use all of the disc or partition for the swap file. Operate the OK button when the changes have been made. This will probably produce a warning message, but it is safe to go ahead with the changes provided you have been careful not to make any careless errors.

System Restore

The System Restore facility of Windows ME and Windows XP is a very useful one, but it requires compressed copies of old system files to be retained so that the operating system can be returned to an earlier state. Automatically adding restoration points obviously takes up time, and the copies of old system files can eventually take up a large amount of disc space. Despite the usefulness of the System Restore facility, some users prefer to switch it off in order to conserve system resources. This does remove an escape route if the operating system becomes seriously damaged, but the System Restore feature is far from essential where a full backup of the main drive is available.

In order to switch off the System Restore feature in Windows ME it is first a matter of going to the Windows Control Panel. Double-click the System icon and then operate the Performance tab when the

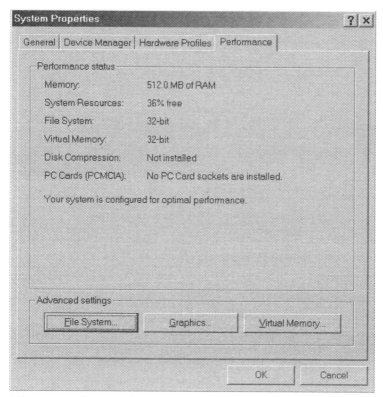

Fig.4.38 The Performance section of System Properties

System Properties window appears (Figure 4.38). Next the File System button is operated, and this produces the File System Properties window of Figure 4.39. Operating the Troubleshooting tab produces a page that has a number of checkboxes (Figure 4.40). In this case it is the one at the bottom that is of interest, and ticking this box disables the System Restore feature. Operate the OK button to make the change take effect.

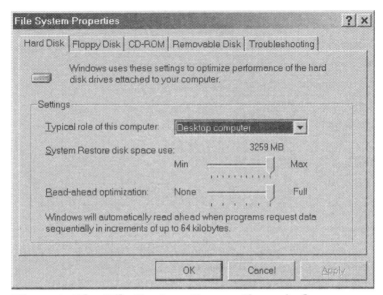

Fig.4.39 The File System Properties window

In Windows XP it is again a matter of first going to
the Control Panel and double-clicking the System
icon. This produces a System Properties window like
the one in Figure 4.41. Operate the System Restore
tab to produce the page shown in Figure 4.42. Tick
the checkbox near the top of the window and then
operate the Apply and OK buttons to make the change
take effect.

Drivers

In an ideal world the manufacturers of computer
hardware such as video and audio cards would supply
the perfect drivers with their products. In the real
world very little hardware seems to be launched

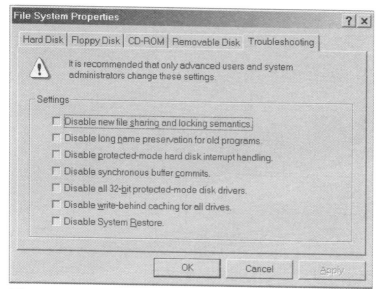

Fig.4.40 The troubleshooting section has a number of checkboxes

complete with fully tested, working, and optimised drivers. In fact it seems to be quite normal for equipment to be launched even though the drivers are not fully operational. Video card manufacturers seem to be particularly bad offenders in this respect.

Consequently, it is worthwhile searching the Internet for newer and better versions of the hardware drivers for your PC. The web site of the computer's manufacturer will often have updated drivers for the hardware used in their PCs. Failing that, it is a matter of going to the web sites of the companies that produced the individual components. Note that drivers are often needed for hardware that is part of

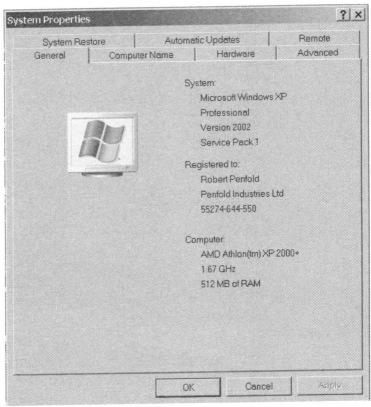

Fig.4.41 The Windows XP System Properties window

the main board, so it is worthwhile investigating the web site of the main board's manufacturer. If you use the Windows Update facility this will often have updates for drivers in addition to the usual security patches, etc.

When looking for new hardware drivers it is necessary to exercise due care. Manufacturers of computer hardware tend to produce a number of products

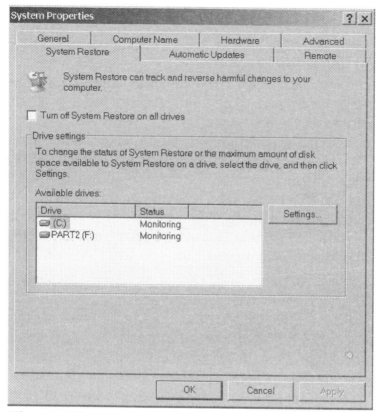

Fig.4.42 The required checkbox is in the System Restore section

under similar names, making it easy to download the wrong drivers. Installing the wrong hardware could make the computer unusable, although reverting to the original drivers should solve the problem. This can be more difficult than one might expect, and it is certainly something that should be avoided.

Modem efficiency

If you have Internet access via a dialup connection it is unlikely that you will be satisfied with the connection speed. There are programs that enable large downloads to be handled more efficiently, and others that will tweak certain Windows Registry settings in an attempt to provide speedier downloads. There is also the option of tweaking the Windows Registry yourself in an attempt to optimise results, but direct editing of the Registry is not something to be undertaken lightly. Get it wrong and you could end up with a PC that operates unreliably or will not boot into Windows at all.

The two Registry tweaks that are normally used to improve results with modems are the MTU and MSS settings. MTU stands for Maximum Transmission Unit, and it sets the maximum size for a packet of data. It is normally set at 1500 bytes, which is fine for a local area network (LAN). It can be too high for use with a dial-up modem, giving reduced performance.

Although the packet size may seem to be of no great consequence, you have to bear in mind that with this type of link it is not unusual for errors to occur. The system includes error checking, and this does not give problems with corrupted data. If a packet contains errors that can not be corrected, the whole packet is sent again. Taking an extreme example, with a packet size of one million bytes, an error free packet might never be received. At the other extreme, taking things on a byte by byte basis would waste a lot of time regulating the flow of data. What is needed is a good compromise between these two extremes.

Another train of thought about MTU is that setting it too large results in packets of data to or from your PC being larger than the packet size used by your Internet service provider. This results in the packets being broken down into smaller packets and then reassembled at the destination, which reduces efficiency. Whichever way you look at it, a smaller packet size can be beneficial.

The MSS (Maximum Segment Size) value controls the maximum amount of data that can be sent in a packet. At first sight it may seem that this is the same as the MTU value, but you have to bear in mind that each packet actually contains more than the data. For example, it contains addresses that enable it to find its way from the server to your PC. Consequently, the MSS value is slightly smaller than the one for the MTU setting.

Tweaking

You can tweak these registry values using either the Windows Regedit program or a special utility program. The Regedit method has the advantage of avoiding the need to buy any additional software, but you do have to proceed very carefully in order to avoid damaging the system. Any alterations to the Registry are made at your own risk. It is always a good idea to make backup copies of the existing registry files before making any changes.

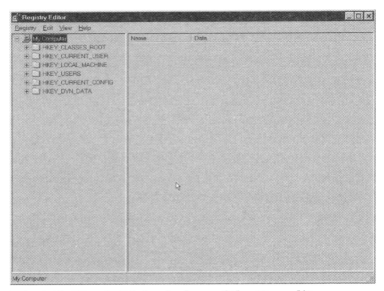

*Fig.4.43 The initial window of the Regedit
        program*

The first task is to find the section of the registry that
deals with the dialup adapter. Start the Registry
Editor program by selecting Run from the Start menu.
Then type "regedit" into the text box and operate the
OK button. This will launch the Regedit program,
which will have an initial window like the one
in Figure 4.43.   Next left-click on the
HKEY_LOCAL_MACHINE folder. This should result
in something like Figure 4.44. Then expand the
Enum, Root, and Net folders so that you have
something like Figure 4.45. Every PC is different, so
the exact Registry entries may be different on your
PC, but there should be several subfolders of the Net
folder with names like 000, 0001, 0002, etc.

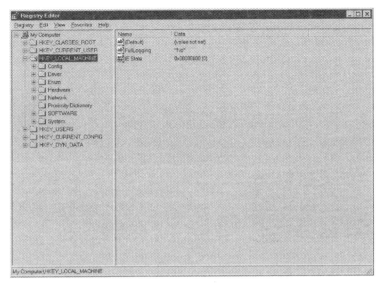

Fig.4.44 Expanding HKEY_LOCAL_MACHINE

Now left-click on each of these folders in turn, and look at the data that appears in the right-hand section of the window. You are looking for the entry that has "DeviceDesc" in the Name field and "Dial-Up Adapter" in the Data field. This will probably be found in the first of the folders (Figure 4.46). The folder that contains this entry should have a subfolder called Bindings, which should now be expanded. This subfolder should contain an Entry in the name field that starts "MSTCP/", followed by a four-digit number. Make a note of this number, which will probably just be 0000 (Figure 4.47). Next go to:

HKEY_LOCAL_MACHINE\Enum\Network\MSTCP\xxxx

Here xxxx is the four-digit number noted previously. In this folder there should be a Value entry called

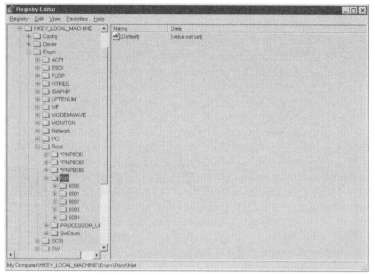

Fig.4.45 Expand the Enum, Root, and Net folders

Driver, and its Data entry will be something like
"NetTrans0000" (Figure 4.48). It is the four-digit
number in the Data entry that is required.

Close the subfolders to remove the clutter in the left-
hand side of the screen and return to the basic keys.
To make the changes to the Registry go to
HKEY_LOCAL_MACHINE again and go down the
directory structure through Syste,CurrentControlSet,
Services, Class, NetTrans, and 000x. Here 000x is the
number of the dialup adapter that you determined
previously, or 0000 in this example. This should give
you something like Figure 4.49. Right-click in the
right-hand section of the screen to produce a small
popup menu (Figure 4.50) and select the String Value
option. A new Value entry then appears in the list

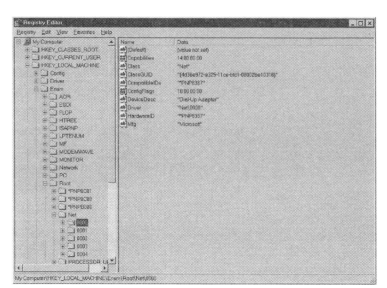

Fig.4.46 Find the subfolder with "DeviceDesc" in the Name field

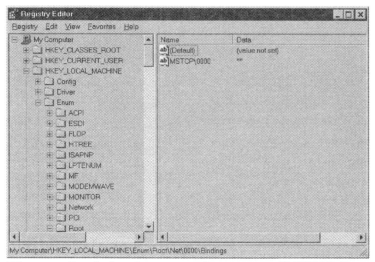

Fig.4.47 Look for the entry that starts "MSTCP"

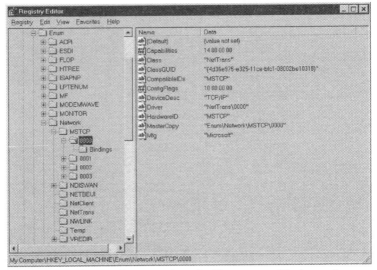

Fig.4.48 The Driver entry is the one of interest

(Figure 4.51), and this is edited to read "MaxMTU". Then double-click on the new entry to produce the window of Figure 4.52 where a value of 576 should be entered. Repeat this process, but the second time use "MaxMSS" for the Value field and 536 as the Data value. Next choose Exit from the File menu to close Regedit and then reboot the computer so that the changes can take effect. Run Regedit again and check that the changes are present and correct (Figure 4.53). Close Regedit and go online to see if the new settings have the desired effect.

There are no entries for MTU and MSS already present in the Registry because the default values are built into the Windows program code and are not

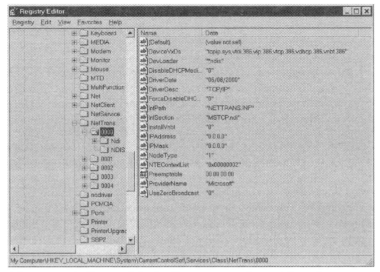

*Fig.4.49 At last, this is the page where the changes
are made*

normally controlled by way of the Registry. Thus the
entries first have to be generated and then given data
values. If you find entries for MTU and MSS already
present, either
someone has
already added
them manually
or they have
been placed
there by
an accelerator
program.

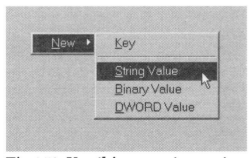

Note   that
tweaking MTU

*Fig.4.50 Use this menu to create
a new string value*

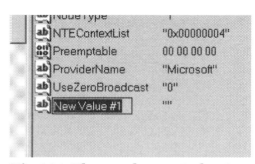

Fig.4.51 The newly created entry

and MSS must be repeated for each dialup adapter if there is more than one installed. There will almost certainly be more than one if you are using two or more Internet service provider. Additional adapters will be found in the keys called 0001, 0002, etc., when initially searching the Registry for the main dialup adapter's entry.

Internet advice

There are endless Windows and hardware tweaks detailed on the Internet, and it is worthwhile searching for the latest tweaks if the ultimate in performance is important to you. Many of these tweaks are specific to certain hardware such as a

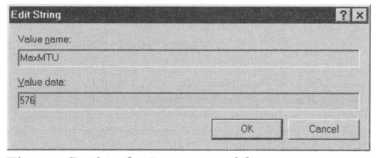

Fig.4.52 Setting the Data part of the new entry

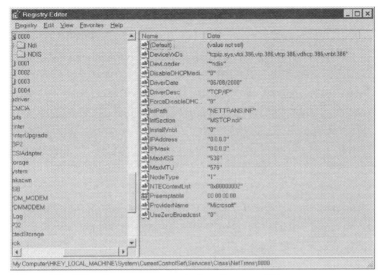

Fig.4.53 The two new entries in position

particular graphics card. This is fine if you happen to be using the appropriate hardware, but it clearly means that many of the ideas will not be relevant to your particular PC.

Bear in mind that many of the ideas for tuning items of hardware involve some form of over-clocking. In other words, they involve running some of the hardware beyond its normal limits. If you should happen to "fry" some of the chips in your PC there will be no prospect of getting replacements under guarantee. You do this type of thing entirely at your own risk.

It is also important to bear in mind that some of the advice available on the Internet is less than totally reliable. In some cases the advice is just poorly explained, rendering it either useless or even potentially harmful. There is also a percentage that is deliberately misleading, and this type of thing will usually attempt to make users do something that will damage their PCs. It is not advisable to take anything on the Internet at face value, and this is certainly the case with PC tweaks.

Points to remember

Windows includes some useful tools and facilities for keeping a PC running efficiently. The Disk Cleanup utility is a quick way of removing certain types of clutter from the hard disc. As with any cleanup utility, it is possible to remove something useful from the disc. A certain amount of care should be exercised when using it.

One of the main causes of a PC gradually slowing down is fragmentation of the files on the hard disc. Windows includes a defragmenter program, and running this occasionally should keep the hard drive operating efficiently.

It is worth running Scandisk (Windows ME) or Check Disk (Windows XP) when a PC seems to take an eternity each time the hard disc is accessed. There could be a flaw in the filing system which these utilities will detect and correct.

Over a period of time it is quite normal for a PC to have more and more programs installed. This can lead to a gradual slowing down, and it is advisable to uninstall any unused programs if a PC suffers a serious case of software bloat. Always use a proper uninstaller to remove unwanted programs and do not simply delete their folders.

Background processes can seriously slow down a PC. Each process will probably consume only a small amount of memory and processor time, but the cumulative effect of several processes can be very significant. Some processes perform vital tasks, but there are usually a few that can be switched off without any ill effects.

Cookies are small text files used by some web sites to provide facilities such as logging in automatically. Huge numbers of them can accumulate on the hard disc and it is advisable to clear them from time to time. Deleting all the cookies might result in a loss of facilities at some web sites, but it should not take long to reinstate these facilities.

Applications that use a lot of memory, and eventually resort to virtual memory, will run faster if a separate swap file is used. Ideally this should be on a separate hard drive to the system files, etc., and used for nothing else. Failing that, its own partition on drive C should suffice.

Tweaking a couple of Registry entries can give a slight improvement in the speed of dialup Internet access. However, directly editing the Registry is not a good idea unless you have a reasonable understanding of what you are doing.

Uninstalling
programs

Deleting files

As explained in the previous chapter, Windows has built-in facilities that can help you to remove certain types of file that are no longer required, but there is a limit to the scope of these facilities. They can not, for instance, manage your data files for you. Only you know which data files are likely to be needed in the future and should be retained on the hard disc drive. The rest can be copied onto some form of removable media before they are deleted from the disc. Of course, it is not essential to make archive copies if you are sure that the files will never be needed again, but it is advisable to take copies "just in case".

You could try erasing programs and other files that are no longer needed, but this type of thing has to be undertaken with great care. In the days of MS/DOS it was perfectly acceptable to delete a program and any files associated with it if you no longer wished to use the program. Matters are very different with Windows, where most software is installed into the operating system.

There are actually some simple programs that have just one file, and which do not require any installation. These standalone program files are quite rare these days, but they can be used much like old MS/DOS programs. To use the program you copy it onto the hard disc, and to run it you use the Run option from the Start menu, or locate the file using Windows Explorer and double-click on it. No installation program is used, and it is perfectly all right to remove the program by deleting the program file.

Probably the easiest way to delete a file or folder using Windows is to locate the item using Windows Explorer, and then right-click on its entry to produce a pop-up menu. Select Delete from this menu (Figure 5.1) and then operate the Yes button when asked if you are sure that you wish to delete it. An item can also be deleted by left-clicking its entry to select it, and then operating the Delete key. Again, operate the Yes button when asked if you are sure that you wish to delete the item.

With either method, multiple items can be selected by holding down the Control key and then left-clicking each item for deletion. A block of files can be selected by left-clicking the first entry, holding down the Shift key, and then left-clicking the last entry in the block.

Most programs are installed onto the computer using an installation program, and this program does not simply make folders on the hard disc and copy files into them from the CD-ROM. It will also make changes to the Windows configuration files so that the program is properly integrated with the operating

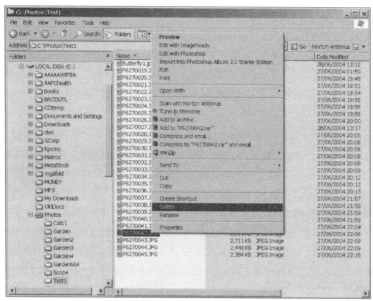

Fig.5.1 Files are easily deleted using Windows Explorer

system. If you simply delete the program's directory structure to get rid of it, Windows will not be aware that the program has been removed. During the boot-up process the operating system will probably look for files associated with the deleted program, and will produce error messages when it fails to find them.

Matters are actually more involved than this, and there is another potential problem in that Windows utilizes shared files. This is where one file is shared by two or more programs, and it is usually DLL (dynamic link library) files that give problems. A DLL file contains program code that is used to provide the main program with additional features. Windows itself utilises large numbers of these files, which are also available for application programs to use. Practically every time you install a program on your PC, it will have its own entourage of new DLL files. These might be made available to and used by other programs.

In deleting a program and the other files in its directory structure, particularly DLL files, you could be deleting files needed by other programs. This could prevent other programs from working properly, or even from starting up at all. If a program is loaded onto the hard disc using an installation program, the only safe way of removing it is to use an uninstaller program. There are three possible ways of handling this.

Custom uninstaller

Some programs load an uninstaller program onto the hard disc as part of the installation process. This program is then available via the Start menu if you choose Programs, and then the name of the program concerned. When you choose this option there will the program itself, plus at least one additional option in the sub-menu that appears. If there is no uninstall option here, no custom uninstaller has been installed for that program. Uninstaller programs of this type are almost invariably automatic in operation, so you have to do little more than instruct it to go ahead with the removal of the program.

With any uninstaller software you may be asked if certain files should be removed. This mostly occurs

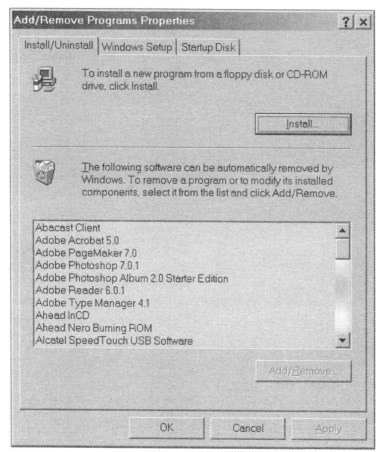

Fig.5.2 The Windows ME uninstaller

where the program finds shared files that no longer
appear to be shared. In days gone by it did not seem
to matter whether you opted to remove or leave these
files, with Windows failing to work properly thereafter!
These days things seem to be more reliable, and it is
reasonably safe to accept either option. To leave the

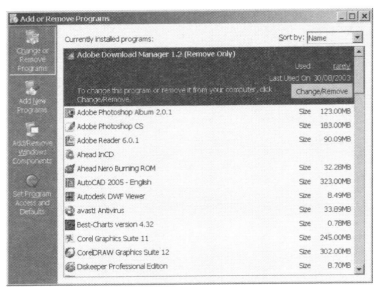

Fig.5.3 The Windows XP version of the uninstaller

files in place is certainly the safest option, but it also results in files and possibly folders being left on the disc unnecessarily.

Windows uninstaller

Windows has a built-in uninstaller that can be accessed via the control panel. From the Start menu select Settings, Control Panel and Add/Remove programs. By default this takes you to the uninstaller, and the lower section of the screen shows a list of the programs that can be uninstalled via this route. Figure 5.2 shows the Windows ME version of the uninstaller, and Figure 5.3 shows the Windows XP equivalent. Although different in points of detail these

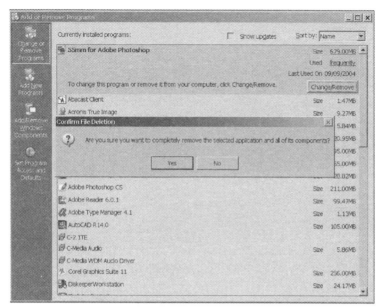

*Fig.5.4 Operate the Yes button to go ahead and
uninstall the program*

two programs are used in much the same way.
Removing a program is just a matter of selecting it
from the list and then operating the Add/Remove
button (Windows ME) or the Change/Remove button
(Windows XP). Confirm that you wish to remove the
program when prompted in the new window that
appears (Figure 5.4), and the removal process will
then begin.

In theory the list should include all programs that
have been added to the hard disc using an installation
program. In practice there may be one or two that
have not been installed "by the book" and can not be
removed using this method. Some programs can only

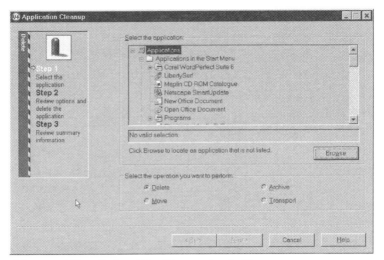

Fig.5.5 The CyberMedia uninstall program

be removed using their own uninstaller program, while others have no means of removal at all. It is mainly older software that falls into the non-removable category, particularly programs that were written for Windows 3.1 and not one of the 32-bit versions of Windows. In fact it is very unusual for old Windows 3.1 software to have any means of removal.

Third party

There are uninstaller programs available that can be used to monitor an installation and then uninstall the software at some later time. As this feature is built into any modern version of Windows, and the vast majority of applications programs now either utilize the built-in facility or have their own uninstaller software, these programs are perhaps less useful than they once were. Most will also assist in the removal of programs that they have not been used to install, and this is perhaps the more useful role. Most will also help with the removal of things like unwanted entries in the Start menu and act as general cleanup software, although Windows itself provides means of clearing some of this software debris. Figure 5.5 shows the CyberMedia Uninstaller program in action, but there are numerous programs of this type to choose from.

Leftovers

Having removed a program by whatever means, you will sometimes find that there are still some files and folders associated with the program remaining on the hard disc. In some cases the remaining files are simply data or configuration files that have been generated while you were trying out the program. If they are no longer of any use to you there should be no problems if they are deleted using Windows Explorer.

In other cases the files could be system files that the uninstaller has decided not to remove in case they are needed by other applications. Sometimes the uninstaller will produce a message stating that it was unable to remove all the files and folders. Often there is no message but a number of files and folders are left behind anyway. Removing files other than your own unwanted data files is obviously more risky, and it is probably better to leave them in place.

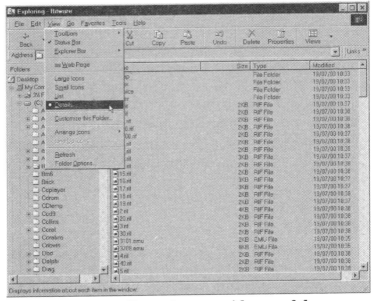

Fig.5.6 The Details option provides useful information about the files

Sometimes the folders may seem to be empty, but it is best to check carefully before removing them. An important point to bear in mind here is that not all files are shown when using the default settings of Windows Explorer. Using the default settings hidden files will live up to their name and files having certain extensions are not shown either.

In normal use this can be helpful because it results in files that are likely to be of interest being shown, while those that are of no interest are hidden. This makes it much easier to find the files you require in a folder that contains large numbers of files. It is clearly unhelpful when looking inside folders to see if they

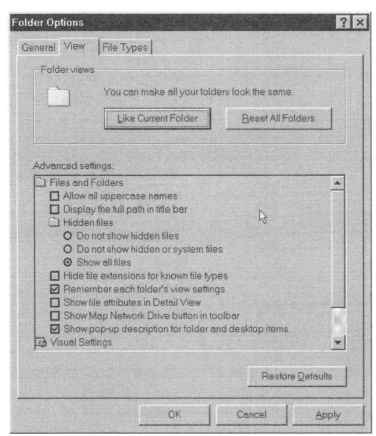

*Fig.5.7 The View section of the Folder Options
window*

contain any files, as it could give the impression that
a folder is empty when it does in fact contain files.
Windows Explorer should be set to show as much
detail about the files as possible.

First go to the View menu and select the Details
option (Figure 5.6). This will result in the size, type,
and date of each file being shown. Then go to the

View menu again, select Folder Options, and then left-click on the View tab in the new Window that appears (Figure 5.7). Under the Hidden Files entry in the main section of the window select the "Show all files" option. The hidden files are certain critical system files, such as those associated with the Windows Registry, that are not normally displayed by Windows Explorer so that they can not be accidentally altered or erased by the user. I would recommend ticking the checkbox for "Display full path in title bar". This way you can always see exactly what folder you are investigating, even if it is one that is buried deep in a complex directory structure.

Remove the tick in the checkbox next to "Hide the extension for known file types". The extension should then be shown for all file types, which makes it easy to see which one is which when several files have the same main file name. When viewing the contents of directories you can use either the List or Details options under the View menu, but the Details option provides a little more information. It provides the file type if it is a recognised type, and the date that the file was created or last altered. If the "Show attributes in Detail view" checkbox is ticked, it will also show the attribute of the file. These are the letters used for each of the four attributes:

A   **Archive**

H   **Hidden**

R   **Read-only**

S   **System**

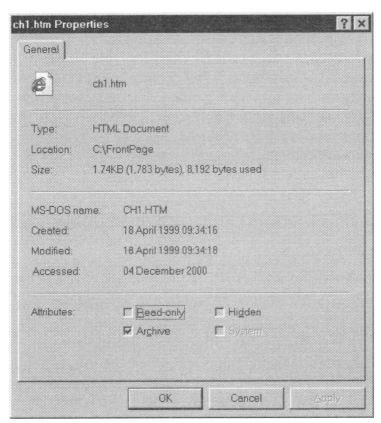

Fig.5.8 The Properties window for a file

Thus a file that has "R" as its attribute letter it is a read-only type, and one that has "HA" in the attribute column is a hidden archive file. Choose the List option if you prefer to have as many files as possible listed on the screen. Details of any file listed can be obtained by right-clicking on its entry in Windows Explorer and then choosing the Properties option from the pop-up menu. This will bring up a screen of the type shown in Figure 5.8, which shows the type of file, the creation date, when it was last modified, size, etc.

Make sure that the checkbox for the "Remember each folder's view settings" is not ticked. Placing a tick in this box gives each folder its own settings, making it necessary to alter the settings for individual folders rather than altering them globally.

If any folders are definitely empty, there should be no problem if they are removed. The same is true of data and configuration files that are no longer needed. With other files it may not be clear what their exact purpose is, and it is a bit risky removing files of unknown function.

Unfortunately, it is not uncommon for uninstallers to leave large numbers of files on the hard disc. The uninstaller seems to go through its routine in standard fashion, and reports that the program has been fully removed, but an inspection of the hard disc reveals that a vast directory structure remains. I have encountered uninstallers that have left more than 50 megabytes of files on the disc, removing only about 10% of those initially installed.

Other uninstallers report that some files and folders could not be removed, and that they must be dealt with manually. Some uninstallers seem to concentrate on extricating the program from the operating system by removing references to the program in the Windows registry, etc., rather than trying to remove all trace of it from the hard disc.

Softly, softly

So what do you do if the disc is left containing vast numbers of unwanted files after a program has been uninstalled? The temptation, and what many people actually do, is to simple drag the whole lot into the Recycle Bin. Sometimes this may be acceptable, but there is the risk that sooner or later Windows will look for some of the deleted files and start to produce error messages. If you are lucky, the deleted files will still be in the Recycle Bin, and they can then be restored to their original locations on the hard disc. If not, you may have problems sorting things out.

The safer way of handling things is to leave the directory structure and files intact, but change some file or folder names. If only a few files have been left behind, try adding a letter at the front of each filename. For example, a file called "drawprog.dll" could be renamed "zdrawprog.dll". This will prevent Windows from finding the file if it should be needed for some reason, but it is an easy matter for you to correct things by removing the "z" from the filename if problems occur.

If there are numerous files in a complex directory structure to deal with it is not practical to rename all the individual files. Instead, the name of the highest folder in the directory structure should be renamed. This should make it impossible for Windows to find the file unless it does a complete search of the hard disc, and it is easily reversed if problems should occur. Ideally the complete directory structure should be copied to a mass storage device such as a CD writer, a backup hard disc drive, or another partition on the hard disc. The original structure can then be deleted. If problems occur and some of the files have been cleaned from the Recycle Bin, you can reinstate everything from the backup copy.

Of course, in cases where little has been left behind by an uninstaller there is not a great deal to be gained by removing a few files of unknown function. Erasing them will not recover much disc space or give a significant increase in performance. It could cause problems in the future if one of the files proves to be important, so this type of disc tidying is probably more trouble than it is worth. The situation is very different where masses of files have been left behind, and it is then worthwhile making some tests to see if they can be removed safely.

Desktop icons

After uninstalling a program you will often find that the shortcut icon is still present on the Windows desktop. If the installation program did not put the icon there in the first place it will not remove it. Shortcut icons that are placed on the Windows desktop manually must be removed manually. This simply entails dragging the icon to the Recycle Bin. There is no risk of this having an adverse effect on Windows operation.

An uninstaller should remove the entry in the Programs section of the Start menu when removing

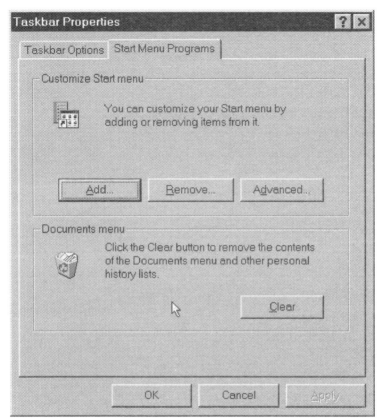

Fig.5.9 The Taskbar Properties window includes a section for the Start menu

a program. Unfortunately, this item does sometimes seem to be overlooked, and after removing a number of programs there can be a growing band of orphan entries in the menu. Once again, removing these entries manually should not entail any risk of "gumming up" Windows, but will make it quicker and easier to use the PC.

225

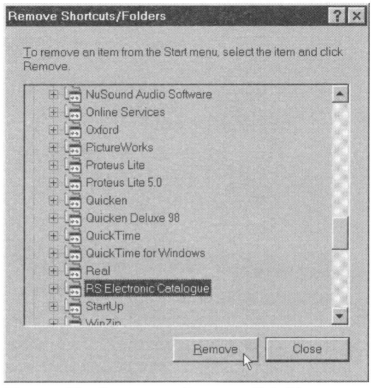

Fig.5.10 The Start menu items are listed here

Menu editing

To remove an orphan entry when using Windows ME, go to Settings in the Start menu, and then select Taskbar and Start Menu. The Taskbar menu is offered by default, so left-click the Start Menu tab to bring up the Window of Figure 5.9. Next left-click on the Remove button, which will bring up a scrollable list of all the items in the Start menu. Left-click on

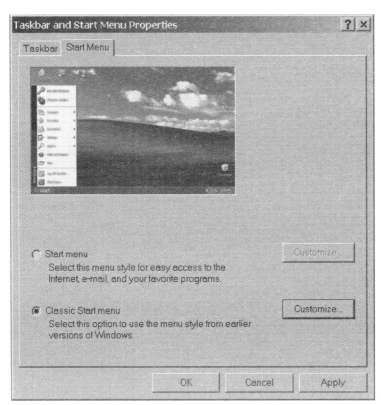

Fig.5.11   The Windows XP version of the Taskbar and Start Menu Properties window

the item you wish to remove in order to highlight it (Figure 5.10), and then left-click the Remove button.

A warning message will appear onscreen to give you a chance to change your mind, and the entry will be deleted if you confirm that you wish to go ahead. A quick check of the Start menu should show that the offending entry has been removed. It is actually

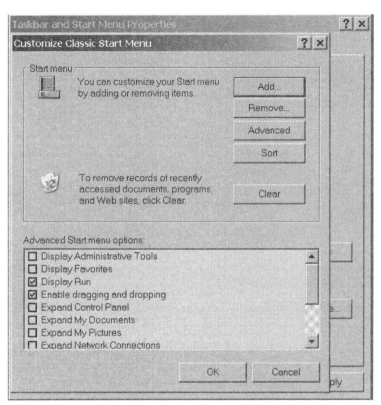

Fig.5.12 Operating the Customize button produces a new window

placed in the Recycle Bin, so it can be easily reinstated if you make a mistake.

Removing an orphan entry from the start menu is slightly different when using Windows XP. The Start Menu section of the Taskbar and Start Menu Properties windows looks like Figure 5.11. Operate the Customize button to produce an additional window (Figure 5.12), and then operate the Remove

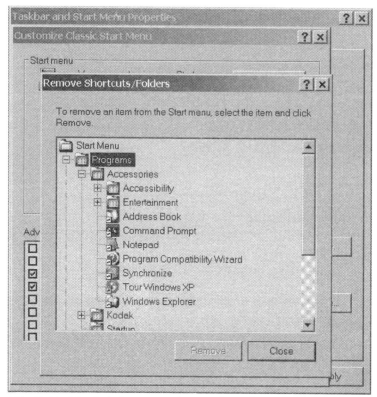

Fig.5.13 To delete an entry, select it and operate the Remove button

button in the new window. The window of Figure 5.13 then pops up. Entries can be selected and then deleted by operating the Remove button.

Points to remember

Deleting data files or other user generated files that are no longer needed should be perfectly safe. However, it is a good idea to make copies of the files on CDR discs first, just in case you need them again at some time in the future.

It is not a good idea to remove programs by simply deleting the relevant files and folders. This can confuse Windows, which will still be set up as if the programs were installed. There could be error messages as a result of this, especially at start-up.

Another potential problem with manual deletion of programs is that Windows allows the use of shared files. When deleting files associated with one program you might also be deleting files required by other programs. This can result in error messages when running the affected programs, or they might simply fail to work at all.

Some programs have an uninstaller that can be accessed via the appropriate submenu in the Programs section of the Start menu. In other cases it should be possible to uninstall the software by using the Add/Remove Programs facility in the Windows Control Panel.

Programs that are uninstalled in the correct fashion should only remove files that are no longer needed by any programs. Nevertheless, if asked if you would like to remove shared files that are no longer needed by other programs you can "play safe" and opt to leave them in place.

Few uninstaller programs remove all the files associated with the uninstalled software. In some cases it is only user-generated files that are left on the hard disc, and these can be deleted if you no longer need them. It is a little risky to remove any other "leftovers" unless you really know what you are doing.

Shortcut icons are sometimes left on the Windows desktop after software has been uninstalled. These can be deleted by dragging them to the Recycle Bin. Occasionally an uninstalled program's entry in the Programs section of the Start menu will also be left in place. This can be deleted via the special facilities that are accessed via the Settings menu.

5   Uninstalling programs

Tuning programs

Be realistic

There are plenty of third-party tuning programs for those that feel the built-in tuning facilities of Windows are inadequate. It is only fair to point out that some of the claims for these programs are a bit unrealistic. In fact the claims for some of them totally lack credibility. If you decide to invest in this type of software it is important to be realistic in your expectations and avoid programs that offer "the earth".

There is also something to be said for sticking with the well-established programs from well-known software houses. A badly written tuning program can easily result in Windows being brought to a halt rather than speeded up. In fact one careless error in an otherwise well-written program could have dire results for a Windows installation. The popular programs are well tried and tested, and should be free from any significant bugs. They will not boost the performance of your PC by 200 percent, but they should help to keep it running efficiently, which is all you can reasonably ask of them.

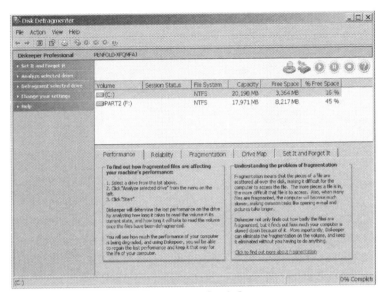

Fig.6.1 The initial screen of Diskeeper 8

Better defragmenting

The benefits of defragmenting a hard disc were covered in chapter 4. Defragmenter programs are available if you feel that something more potent than the built-in utility is required. Probably the most popular of these is Diskeeper, and Figure 6.1 shows the initial screen obtained when running Diskeeper 8. This program is essentially the same as the one supplied with Windows XP, and it will actually install itself in place of the built-in defragmenter when it is installed on a Windows XP system.

The basic defragmenting routine is presumably the same as the one used in the built-in program, but the user interface is rather different. There are buttons

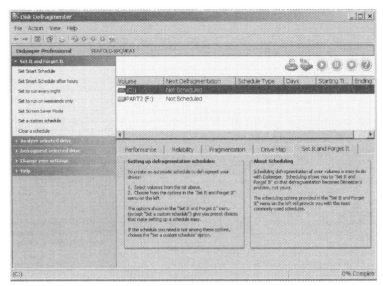

*Fig.6.2 The program can be scheduled to run
automatically if required*

towards the top right-hand corner of the window that
provide shortcuts to some facilities. The bottom
section of the window provides more information than
in the basic program, and some extra features are
available from the menu near the top left-hand corner
of the window.

One of these is the Set and Forget facility (Figure 6.2),
which enables the program to run automatically at
nights, weekends, etc. It is also possible to analyse
the disc at any time (Figure 6.3) and to defragment it
on demand. As with the basic version, the disc will
be placed in efficient working order without
necessarily fully defragmenting the disc (Figure 6.4).

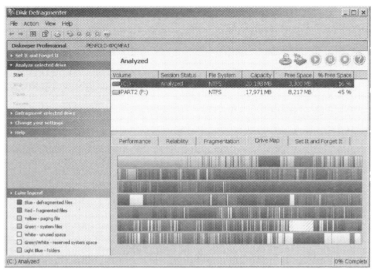

Fig.6.3 The disc can be analysed at any time

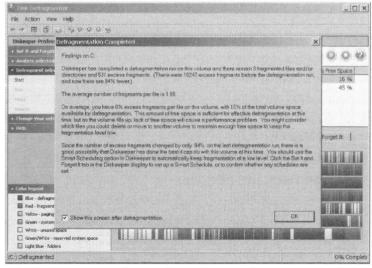

*Fig.6.4 A report is produced once the program has
completed its task*

Buying a disc defragmenter is perhaps a more worthwhile proposition for those running Windows ME than it is for those using Windows XP. A program such as Diskeeper 8 is a large step-up from the Windows ME defragmenter, but it has relatively little advantage for Windows XP users. Whether you opt for the built-in program or a third-party add-on, make sure that you do actually use the program and avoid letting the disc get badly defragmented. A fragmented disc is more or less guaranteed to slow down any program that requires frequent disc accesses.

Easy tweaking

Tweaking the MTU and MSS settings in the Windows Registry was covered in chapter 4. If you do not wish to delve into the Windows Registry directly, and I would certainly not recommend it, the easy alternative is to use one of the many programs that make it easy to change the default values. Here the popular TweakDUN program will be used as an example of this type of acceleration program. This should be available from any of the large software download sites or the manufacturer's site at:

www.pattersondesigns.com.

Unregistered versions of the program are only partially operational, but do enable the MTU and MSS settings to be changed. When first run there is a splash screen followed by a menu that permits the desired adapter to be selected (Figure 6.5). The

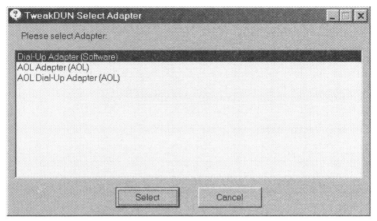

Fig.6.5 Here the appropriate adapter is chosen

adapters listed here will obviously depend on the set-up of your PC. Left-click on the entry for the adapter you wish to modify and then operate the Select button. The program then moves to the main screen (Figure 6.6) where the MTU value of 576 can be selected using the appropriate radio button. Operate the OK button to implement the changes and then the Yes button when asked if you wish to restart the computer. Once the computer has rebooted the changes will have taken effect and it is ready for testing online. This method is certainly a lot easier than manually delving around in the Windows Registry, and it should be equally effective.

General tweaking

There are numerous programs that aid the user to tweak a particular aspect of a PC's performance, and there also a number of all-in-one programs that cover

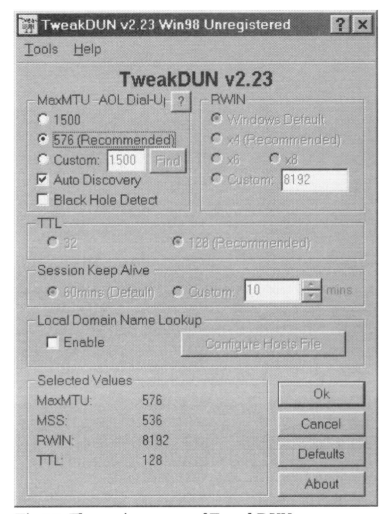

Fig.6.6 The main screen of TweakDUN

many aspects of a PC's performance. The second
category is by far the most popular, and it is certainly
more practical to use one far-ranging program than

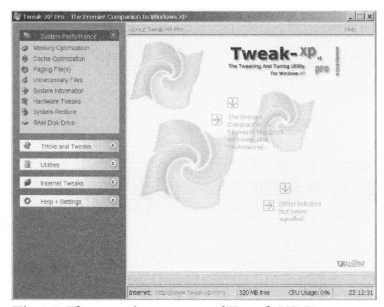

Fig.6.7 The opening screen of Tweak XP Pro

a number of small utilities. On the face of it, specialist programs could provide a performance advantage over a "jack of all trades" program, but in practice the two types of program perform essentially the same tasks. Consequently, any improvement in performance is likely to be much the same whatever program is used to provide the tweaking.

The Tweak.... series of programs is extremely popular, and Figure 6.7 shows the opening screen of Tweak XP Pro. This is a general tune-up program for computers running Windows XP. The range of facilities on offer is so wide that it is broken down into four groups that are accessed via the large menu

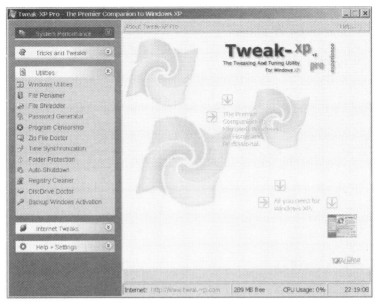

Fig.6.8   The Utilities section includes a Registry cleaner

down the left-hand side of the window. The fifth group gives access to the Help system and the program's own settings. Some of the facilities offered by this program are things such as file shredders that are not anything to do with tuning a PC, but a full range of tuning utilities is also included.

A Registry Cleaner option is available in the Utilities section (Figure 6.8), and this is a useful feature that is to be found in many general tune-up programs. Selecting this option changes the window to look like Figure 6.9, and operating the Start Search button initiates a scan of the Registry. Eventually a list of suspected errors will be listed in the lower section of

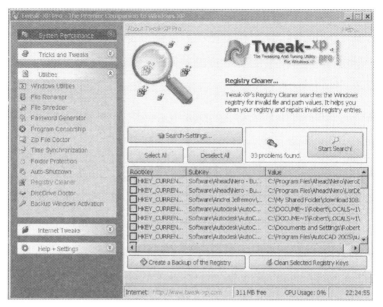

Fig.6.9 A list of erroneous entries is produced

the window, and in this example 33 suspected problems were found. Why does the Registry need cleaning, and what sort of errors will be found?

In theory, there should be no need for any maintenance of the Registry. When software is installed on a PC it makes additions to the Registry. In the days of MS-DOS it was normal for each program to have a folder in which it stored a configuration file or files. A configuration file is a database that contains default settings for the program, such as the screen colours and the default font details. Normal configuration files are little used with modern versions of Windows. Instead, the configuration information is stored in the Registry files, which is where the configuration information for Windows itself is also stored.

Programs should only place valid entries in the Registry during installation. In the real world mistakes are made, and there can be entries that refer to files that do not exist, files that are not in the specified location, and this type of thing. Probably the majority of errors occur when a program is uninstalled. All the Registry entries for a program should be removed when it is uninstalled, but in practice it is quite normal for some entries to be left behind. Sometimes this is done deliberately so the program can use the old configuration settings if it is ever reinstalled. In other cases it is due to deficiencies in the uninstaller program. Either way, there can be entries that serve no useful purpose and simply bloat what is likely to be a huge Registry.

Safety first

Great care needs to be taken when making changes to the Registry manually, since an error could prevent an applications program from running properly. Worse still, an error could give problems with the operating system or even prevent the computer from booting at all. Manually searching the Registry for errors is difficult and time consuming, even if you know what you are doing. Without expert knowledge it is not really a practical proposition and would be more or less guaranteed to end in disaster. The only practical approach is to use programs that can automatically search the Registry for errors and fix them.

Commercial programs that clean up the Registry almost invariably insist on making a backup copy first. If major damage to the registry should result from the changes made it is then reasonably easy to revert to the old Registry. With Windows ME and Windows XP systems a restoration point might be made instead, or in addition to backing up the Registry. If the Registry should be rendered unusable by the changes made, the Windows Restore program can be used to take things back to their original state. It is definitely not a good idea to use any program that alters the Registry unless there is some easy way of reversing the changes.

Returning to Tweak XP Pro, the "orphan" entries are shown in the lower part of the window so that the user can look through them and check that they do not refer to any currently installed software. In this example the entries all referred to either old versions of programs or to software that had been removed from the system. The checkbox is ticked for each entry that is to be removed. Operating the Select All button will add a tick in all the checkboxes, but only after a warning message has been acknowledged. Operate the Clear Selected Registry Keys to go ahead and remove the selected entries. These entries will be deleted once another warning message has been received (Figure 6.10). The PC is then rebooted to make the changes take effect.

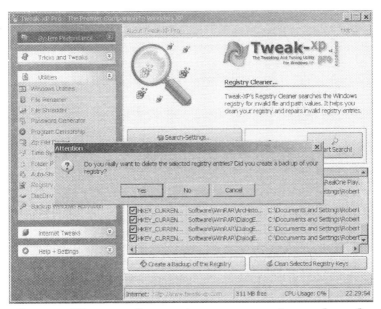

Fig.6.10 The usual warning message is produced before anything is deleted

Some programs search more thoroughly for incorrect Registry entries. Trying TuneUp Utilities on the same PC produced well over four hundred entries that the program considered erroneous in some way. Of course, the more deeply a program delves into the Registry, and the greater the number of changes made, the larger the risk run in permitting the changes. However, letting the TuneUp Utilities program make the additional changes did not produce any problems. Remember that you can always resort to a backup copy of the Registry if major problems are experienced with the "cleaned" version.

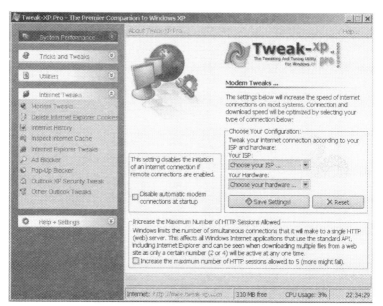

Fig.6.11 The program can tweak the Internet connection

There are many other facilities available in Tweak XP Pro, such as facilities for tweaking the Internet connection (Figure 6.11). This enables optimum performance to be obtained without having to resort to any manual editing of the Registry. Some of the facilities on offer are really just the ones that are available from within Windows. In fact some of the simpler tuning programs seem to do little more than act as a convenient user interface for launching the built-in Windows disc utilities, etc. Most programs take things at least one stage further and try to provide more convenient versions of the standard Windows utilities. Figure 6.12 shows the StartUp

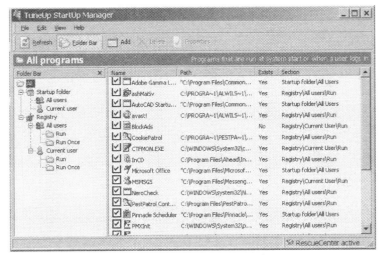

Fig.6.12 The Start-Up manager of the TuneUp program

Manager of the TuneUp program. By default this shows all the programs that are run at start-up so that it is easy to go down the list a remove the tick from the checkbox of any program that you wish to suppress. It is still possible to look at a single category by selecting the appropriate folder in the left-hand section of the window.

Automatic help

Many tuning programs can analyse the system and provide suggestions for improving performance. The initial screen of WinSpeedUp (Figure 6.13 provides access to the usual facilities for clearing the Internet history, emptying the Recycle Bin, and so on, but it also has an automatic analyser. This is in the form of a wizard that can be called up via the menu system.

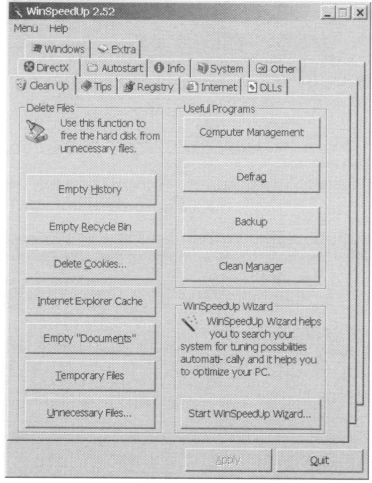

Fig.6.13 The initial screen of WinSpeedUp

It provides a list of items that can be optimised (Figure 6.14), and a tick is placed in the checkbox for any that you wish to go ahead with. It is merely necessary to operate the Next button to go ahead and make the

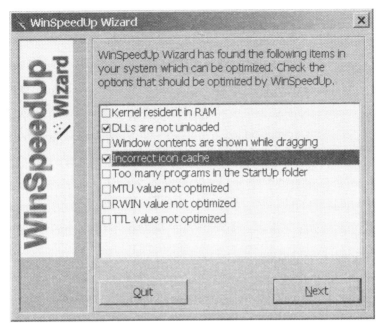

Fig.6.14 A list of improvements is suggested

changes. The changes will not take effect until the
computer has been rebooted, and there is the option
of rebooting immediately (Figure 6.15).

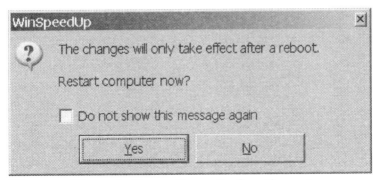

Fig.6.15 There is the option of rebooting at once

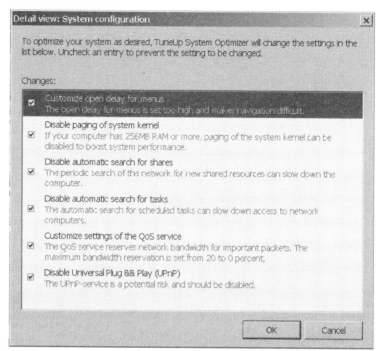

*Fig.6.16 Some suggested improvements from the
         TuneUp program*

The TuneUp program has facilities to analyse various
parts of the system and suggest changes. In Figure
6.16 it has come up with some suggested changes to
the system's configuration. As usual, there is a
checkbox for each suggestion so that you can opt not
to go ahead with any changes that would alter or
remove features that you require. Although there is
an obvious attraction in using a program that alters
the system in a fully automatic fashion, this is not
really something that could be recommended. The
same is true of simply letting the program get on with

it and implement all its suggested changes without bothering to review any of them. It is advisable to check each suggestion and only go ahead with changes that will definitely not nobble a feature that you require.

Memory

It is quite common for tuning programs to include a utility that is intended to provide more effective use of a PC's memory. Separate utilities of this type are also available. When a PC runs out of conventional memory it resorts to using the swap file on a hard disc drive instead. This works, but applications will normally slow down quite significantly when the swap file is used. A memory optimiser tries to prevent the memory from being used up, and it achieves this by removing anything stored in memory that is not considered to be sufficiently important.

Figure 6.17 shows the memory optimiser of the TuneUp program in operation. The display shows how the use of memory changes with time, but this window is normally minimised and the program then runs as a background application. It can be set to optimise the memory usage when a certain key combination is used, and it will then use the manual optimisation setting. This feature is also available from within the program by operating the Manual Optimisation tab followed by the Clear Now button (Figure 6.18). The slider control is used to set the amount of memory that will be cleared. If the

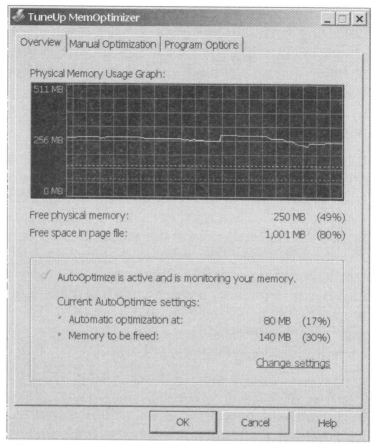

Fig.6.17 The display of the memory optimiser

Windows Clipboard is in use, operating the button in the lower section of the window clears the data stored on the Clipboard.

Of course, a memory optimiser can not work miracles and there is a limit to the effectiveness of any program of this type. If an applications program needs large

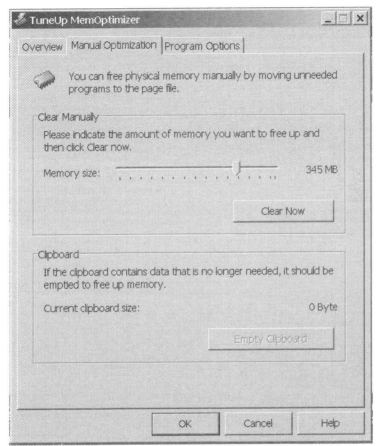

Fig.6.18 Memory can be cleared manually

amounts of memory in order to run efficiently, a small amount of memory plus a memory optimiser is unlikely to give really good results. However, a good memory optimiser will avoid problems such as memory not being freed properly when a program is terminated. It should ensure that good use is made of whatever amount of memory is fitted to the PC.

The optimiser program will itself consume system resources, but it should "earn its keep".

Points to remember

There are plenty of third-party programs that can be used to boost the performance of a flagging PC, but be wary of the inflated claims for some of this software. These programs can help to keep a PC operating at top performance, but they will not turn a 2 gigahertz processor into a 3 gigahertz type.

Third-part disc defragmenters are available, but they will not necessarily do a better job than the built-in program. This is definitely the case with Windows XP, which comes complete with a version of the excellent Diskeeper program. Users of Windows ME perhaps have more to gain by switching to a third-party defragmenter.

Many of the more simple tuning programs seem to do little more than act as a convenient front-end for the built-in facilities of Windows. If you buy this type of software it is advisable to invest in one that offers extra facilities even if this means paying a somewhat higher price.

Registry cleaning programs remove erroneous entries in the Windows Registry. Before using any program that will alter the Registry it is advisable to either make a backup copy of the Registry and (or) create a new restoration point. If the worst should happen it is then relatively easy to return to the original Registry.

Although there are plenty of programs that can provide largely automatic tuning of a PC, the fully automated approach is not the best one. You really need to review the changes that will be made and remove any that will have a detrimental effect on any feature that is of importance to you. You could otherwise end up with an efficient PC that lacks one or two features which you find very useful.

A memory manager or optimiser runs as a background application and it helps to avoid having memory wastage. However, it is no substitute for a large amount of memory when running memory intensive applications.

Backup and Restore

Back to basics

One way of speeding up a bloated Windows installation is to reinstall everything from scratch. This takes things back to a lean installation that lacks the numerous unnecessary files that tend to build up on the hard disc drive, and it will usually produce a less cluttered Registry. It is also an opportunity to completely "lose" any installed software that has proved to be something less than useful. A major drawback of this once popular approach to speeding up a PC is that it can be very time consuming. Modern PCs often have a number of major applications programs installed, together with a selection of small utilities.

Another factor to bear in mind is that most users customise Windows and some of the applications programs. Reinstalling everything from scratch involves redoing any customisation. If you use only a fairly simple setup, then reinstalling everything from scratch remains a practical approach. It is likely to be too time consuming if you use a complex installation that has a great deal of customisation.

Also, there is no guarantee that you will be able to get everything exactly as it was previously. Anyway, reinstalling Windows from scratch is not something that can be recommended for those of limited experience with PCs, and it is not a subject that will be considered further here.

In this chapter a quicker approach is considered, and this is to provide a full backup of a basic installation. In other words, Windows and all the applications software is loaded onto the hard disc, and any customisation is completed. A backup of the hard disc is then taken and this provides a quick means of reverting to the basic installation. Once restored, this installation has all your normal applications and utility programs, all the hardware drivers loaded, and any customisation included. It might be necessary to add or update one or two programs, and any recently produced data will also have to be added, but the total time taken to get back to a fully operational and fast system should be relatively small.

Simply copying all the files on the hard disc to CDRs or another form of mass storage will not enable the system to be restored to its original condition. The files can be copied back to the hard disc, but they will not be in the same places on the restored disc. As a result of this the PC will not be able to boot from the disc. In order to precisely restore a disc to its previous state it is necessary to produce what is termed an image of the disc. It requires special software to produce the image file and restore the disc from this file. Power Quest's Drive Image and Norton's Ghost are two popular programs of this type. There is a rather less sophisticated backup and restore feature included as part of the Windows operating system.

With the current low cost of hard disc drives it is quite common for a large drive to be divided into several partitions. In effect, a large disc becomes two or more smaller discs. One partition is often used to store a backup of the main (boot) partition. Another ploy is to have a second physical drive, which is a clone of the main drive. Either way, any new data placed on the main drive is copied to the backup partition/drive. If the Windows installation is seriously damaged or simply becomes sluggish, it is just a matter of restoring everything from the relevant partition of the backup drive. The PC should then work much as it did before the problem occurred, complete with your data.

Having a second physical drive gives even greater security because it guards against a catastrophic failure of the main drive. If the main drive should fail it is just a matter of installing a new one and installing the backup image onto it. As an emergency measure it is possible to set the backup drive to operate as the boot disc, and you can then go on using the PC while a new disc is obtained.

There is an advantage in having the image filed stored in some form of external storage such as CDRs. This ensures that you have a backup of the system should some form of catastrophic failure result in the hard disc or discs being zapped. It also guards against attack from viruses and other computer pests. Even the most sophisticated of computer viruses is unable to attack files that are on CDRs stored in drawer or cupboard.

Bear in mind though, that a backup on CDR discs will only provide a so-called "snapshot" of your PC at the time the backup copy was made. Going back to the system stored on the CDRs with not restore any data made since the backup was taken. It is therefore important to take copies of data produced since the main backup was taken, so that the data can be copied onto the hard disc once the basic setup has been restored. The program used to make the image of the hard disc might have facilities to backup data made thereafter. If not, it is up to you to ensure that copies of any important data are made onto CDRs or some other form of external storage.

Windows Backup

Using backup programs it is possible to save selected files, directories, directory structures, or the entire contents of the hard disc drive. It should also be possible to make an image of the hard drive so that an exact and bootable copy of it can be restored at a later date. I think I am correct in stating that every version of Windows is supplied complete with a backup program that has the imaginative name of Backup. Although basic compared to some programs of this type it does the job well enough for many users. Its lack of popularity possibly stems from the fact that the equivalent facility in Windows 3.1 was something less than user friendly, causing many users to look elsewhere for a backup utility.

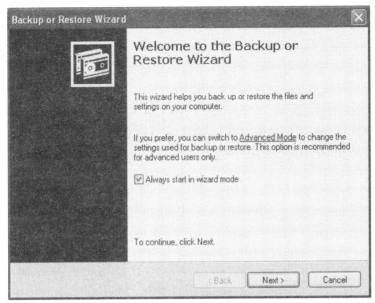

Fig.7.1   The Backup and Restore Wizard

Perhaps the problem is simply that the Backup program is a part of Windows that has often been easy to overlook. Anyway, the Windows XP version is more user-friendly and powerful than previous versions, and it is definitely there if you seek it out. With the Professional version of Windows XP it is installed by default, but with the Home Edition it will probably have to be installed from the Valueadd\Msft\Ntbackup folder on the installation CD-ROM.

Backup Wizard

Once installed, the Backup program is run by selecting All Programs from the Start menu, followed

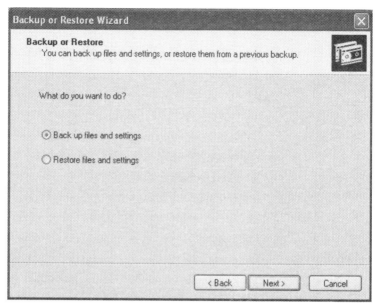

Fig.7.2 This window provides backup and restore options

by Accessories, System Tools, and then Backup. By default the Backup Wizard (Figure 7.1) runs when this program is launched, and initially it is probably best to use the wizard. Operate the Next button to move on to the first stage of using the Backup Wizard (Figure 7.2). Here you have the choice of backing up or restoring data, but it is obviously necessary to produce a backup disc before anything can be restored. Therefore, initially the Backup radio button has to be selected.

The next window (Figure 7.3) is used to select the data to be backed up. The top option produces a backup of the My Documents folder plus some system

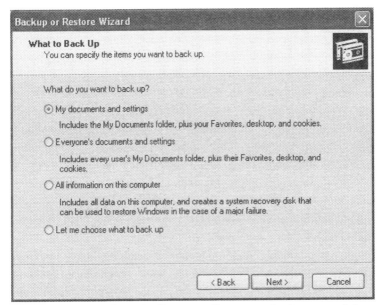

Fig.7/3 Use this window to choose what you wish to backup

settings and cookies. The second option is similar, but it provides a backup of the documents and settings for all users. Using the fourth option produces a file browser (Figure 7.4) so that the user can select the files and folders that will be backed up. The third option is the one that is of most use if the system becomes seriously damaged or the hard disc becomes unusable. It permits the whole system to be backed up, and it also produces a recovery disc that enables it to be easily restored again. In fact the restoration process is almost totally automated. It is the third option that will be considered here.

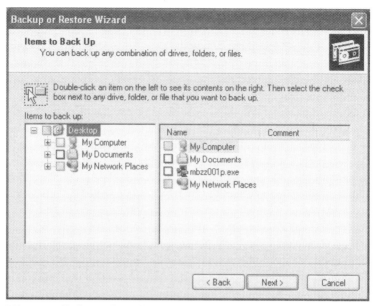

Fig.7.4 Select the files or folders to be backed up

The next window (Figure 7.5) enables the backup
drive to be selected, and a variety of drive types is
supported. These include Zip discs, local hard drives,
and some tape backup systems. Unfortunately, CD
writers are not supported. Sometimes there are ways
of working around this limitation, but it is probably
best to opt for a third party backup program if you
wish to use CD-R or CD-RW discs to hold the backup
files. Use the menu or the Browse option to select
the correct drive. If you select a device that is not
supported by the Backup program, an error message
will be produced when Windows tries to create the
file. This will simply state the backup file could not
be produced.

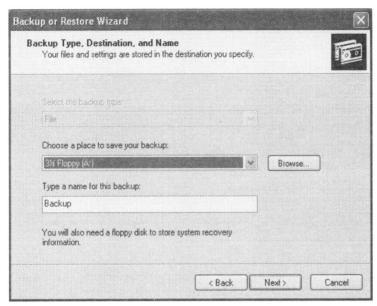

Fig.7.5 Use this window to select the backup drive

In the current context the best option is to have a second drive as the backup device. It is not essential to keep the second drive connected once the backup has been made, and the backup drive can have its power and data leads disconnected once the backup has been completed. Of course, the power should be switched off before the drive is disconnected. The drive is reconnected again if you need to restore the backup copy at some later time. Disconnecting the drive avoids wear and tear, and also keeps the contents safe from viruses. Of course, it also prevents new data from being backed up on the second drive. If you produce large amounts of data it might be

Fig.7.6 The selected options are shown here

worthwhile keeping this drive connected and in operation.

By default, the backup file is called "Backup" but the name in the textbox can be changed to any valid filename. Operating the Next button moves things on to a window like the one in Figure 7.6. This shows the options that have been selected, and provides an opportunity to change your mind or correct mistakes. Use the Back button if it is necessary to return to earlier windows to make changes, or operate the Finish button to go ahead and make the backup file.

A window like the one shown in Figure 7.7 will appear, and this shows the progress made by the Backup

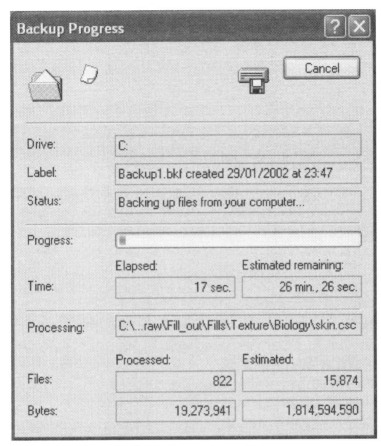

Fig.7.7 This window shows how things are progressing

program. It provides an estimate for the time remaining until the task is completed, and this will vary massively depending on the amount of data to be saved and the speed of the backup device. With many gigabytes of data to backup it is definitely a good idea to use a fast backup device such as a second hard

Fig.7.8 A floppy disc must be inserted in drive A

disc drive. With a slow backup device the process can take many hours. Where appropriate, you will be prompted when a disc change is necessary. With multiple disc backups, always label all the discs clearly. You will then be able supply the right disc each time when restoring the backup copy. Do not worry if the size of the backup file is substantially less than the total amount of data on the hard disc. The backup file is probably compressed, or perhaps no backup copies are made of standard files that are available from the Windows XP installation disc. Anyway, it is quite normal for the backup file to be significantly smaller than the source.

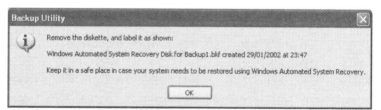

*Fig.7.9 This message indicates that the backup
has been completed*

The message shown in Figure 7.8 will appear towards the end of the backup process. The floppy disc is

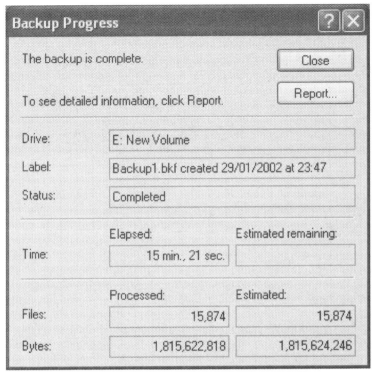

Fig.7.10 Statistics in the Backup Progress window

needed to make an automatic recovery disc. This disc is needed in order to restore the system from the backup disc, and the backup is relatively little value without the recovery disc. Insert a 1.44-megabyte floppy disc into drive A: and operate the OK button. The message of Figure 7.9 appears once the recovery disc has been completed. Label the disc as indicated in the message and store it safely. The automatic recovery process is not possible without this disc. Finally, you are returned to the Backup Progress

7 Backup and Restore

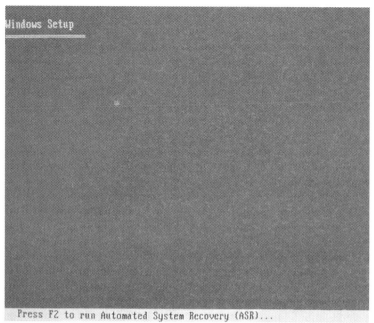

Press F2 to run Automated System Recovery (ASR)...

*Fig.7.11 Press the F2 key as soon as this message
appears at the bottom of the screen*

window (Figure 7.10), which should indicate that the
backup has been completed successfully.

Restoring

There is little point in having a means of restoring
the backup that requires the computer to boot
normally into Windows XP, since this will often be
impossible when the restoration feature is needed.
The Windows XP method of restoring a full system
backup is more straightforward than the Windows 9x
equivalent. In fact the Windows XP method makes
the process about as simple as it is ever likely to be.

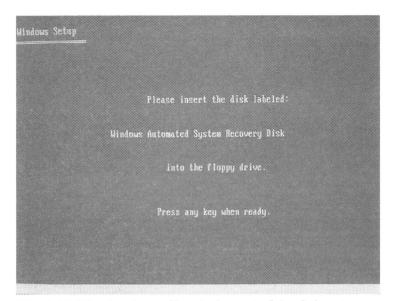

Fig.7.12 The backup disc is inserted in drive A

It is termed the Automated System Recovery, and it certainly lives up the automated part of its name.

The first task is to boot from the Windows XP installation CD-ROM, and the BIOS must be set to boot from the CD-ROM drive before it tries to boot from the hard disc drive. If the boot sequence is the other way around, the computer will probably start to boot from the hard drive and the CD-ROM drive will be ignored. With the installation disc in a CD-ROM drive and the correct BIOS settings, a message saying "Press any key to boot from CD-ROM" will appear for a few seconds at the beginning of the boot process. Press any key while this message is displayed or the computer will revert to booting from the hard disc drive.

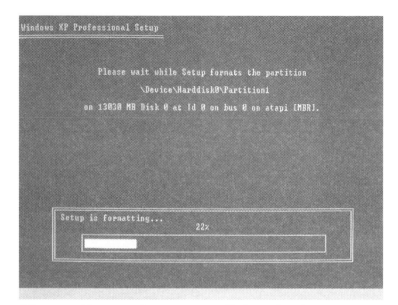

*Fig.7.13   Formatting erases all data in the
            partition*

Messages appear along the bottom of the screen
when the computer starts booting from the CD-ROM.
Look for the one that says "Press F2 to run Automated
System Recovery (ASR)", as in Figure 7.11. This
message only appears briefly, so press F2 as soon as
it appears. After some disc activity the message of
Figure 7.12 will appear, and the floppy disc produced
when backup was made must be placed in drive A:.
Then press any key to continue. The restoration
process requires little intervention from the user, but
it is as well to keep an eye on things in case something
goes wrong. First the partition used by the system is
formatted, which effectively wipes all data from the
partition. If there is any data on the disc that has not

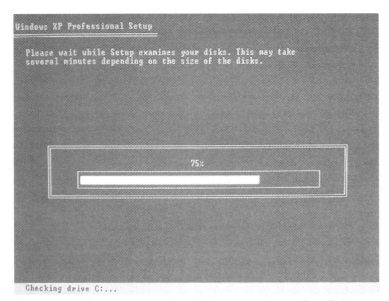

Fig.7.14 The program briefly examines the drives

been backed up, it is lost forever at this stage. The formatting will take several minutes, and an onscreen "fuel gauge" shows how far the formatting has progressed (Figure 7.13).

A similar gauge is used at the next screen (Figure 7.14), where the program examines the disc drives. This is usually much quicker than formatting the restoration partition, and this screen may only appear for a second or two. A further gauge appears on the next screen (Figure 7.15), and here the program copies some files to the hard disc. Next the program loads some more files (Figure 7.16). The computer is then rebooted, and it will reboot after several seconds even if you do not press Return to restart the computer (Figure 7.17).

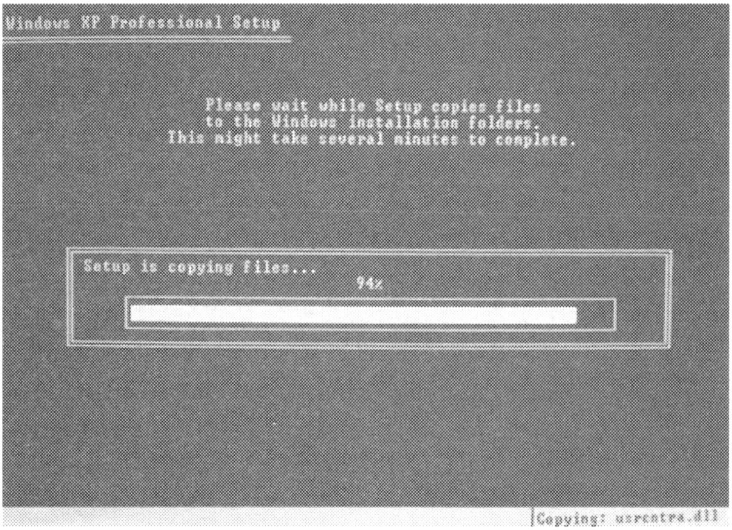

Fig.7.15 The installation files are copied

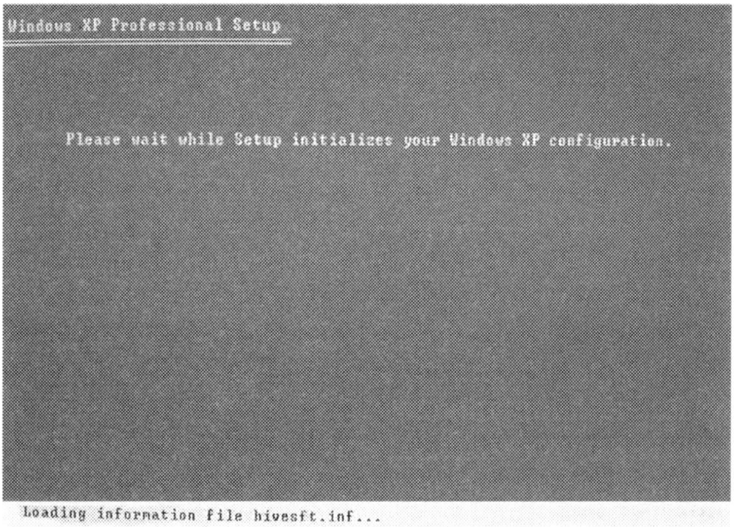

Fig.7.16 Next more files are loaded

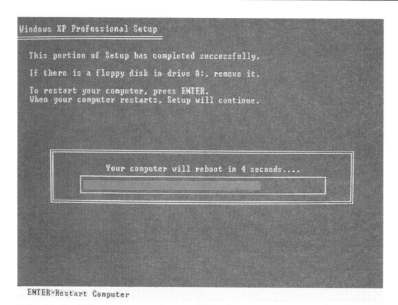

*Fig.7.17   The computer will reboot automatically if
the Return key is not operated*

Note that the Automated System Recovery disc in
drive A: must be removed at this stage. The computer
might try to boot from this disc if it is left in the drive,
and this would probably prevent the computer from
rebooting properly. If the reboot should stall because
the disc is left in drive A:, removing it and pressing
any key should get things underway again.

Windows is installed on the appropriate partition
when the computer has rebooted, and a screen like
the one in Figure 7.18 shows how the installation is
progressing. Once Windows has been installed, the
Automated System Recovery Wizard runs (Figure
7.19). This does not require any input from the user
though, and you can just sit back and watch while your

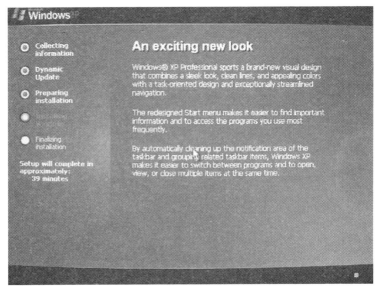

Fig.7.18 Installation now starts in earnest

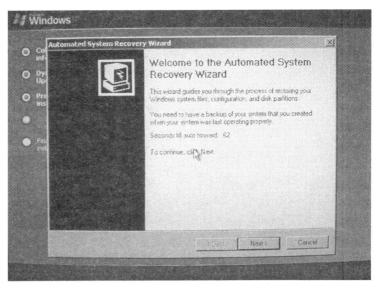

Fig.7.19 The Automatic Recovery Wizard

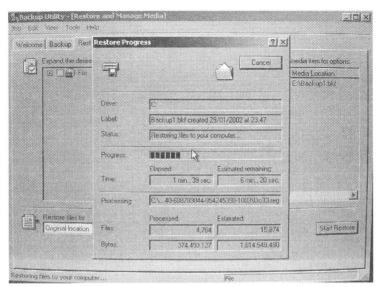

Fig.7.20 *Files are copied to the hard disc*

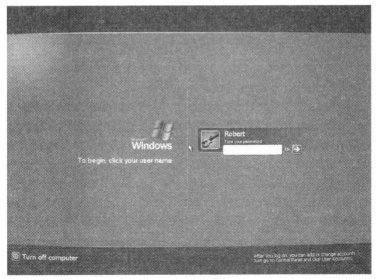

Fig.7.21 *Login once the files have been restored*

Fig.7.22 Windows XP should work as before

files are restored to the hard disc (Figure 7.20). Once this has been completed, the usual login screen (Figure 7.21) appears. You login using your normal password, and the computer then goes into Windows XP (Figure 7.22). This should look the same and have the same settings that were in force when the backup was made. Any programs, data, etc., on the partition that was backed up should be included in the restored installation.

In practice there might be one or two minor differences to the system. In particular, any passwords or other data hidden on the disc in "invisible" files will not have been placed on the backup disc. Files of this type are very secure, but

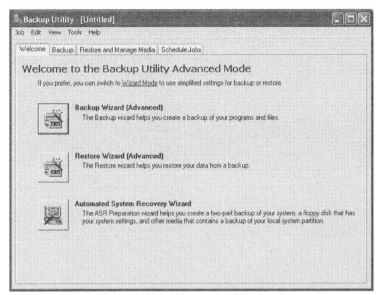

Fig.7.23 Three options are offered when the Advanced mode is selected

they are "invisible" to the Backup program. It is therefore unable to save them in the backup file. This should not be of any major consequence, because the relevant applications can be run, and the passwords (or whatever) can be stored on the hard disc again. Of course, any data files produced after the backup was made will not be automatically restored to the hard disc. They must be restored manually, and it is essential to make sure that any recent data files are backed up before you start the restoration process.

Advanced mode

Use of the Backup Wizard is not mandatory, and the Backup program can be controlled directly by the

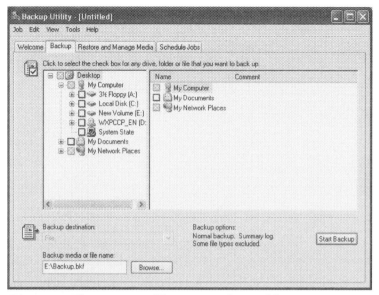

Fig.7.24 The source files are selected here

user. Start running the program in the usual way, but left-click on the "Advanced mode" link. This produces a window like the one in Figure 7.23, and two of the buttons give access to more advanced versions of the Backup and Restore wizards. The third button provides another route to the Automated System Recovery Wizard. The tabs near the top of the window provide manual operation of the Backup and Restore programs, and to scheduled backups.

Figure 7.24 shows the window for the Backup program. The files and folders to be backed up are selected in the upper section of the window, while the backup drive and filename are entered in the textbox near the bottom left-hand corner of the window. The

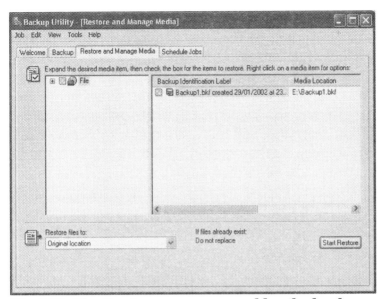

*Fig.7.25 The Restore program enables the backup
file and destination to be specified*

usual Browse facility is available here. Once
everything has been set up correctly, the Start Backup
button is operated. The Restore program's window
is shown in Figure 7.25. The upper section of the
window is used to locate and select the backup file,
and the lower section is used to select the destination
of the restored backup. This will usually be the
original location, but it can be restored to an
alternative location. Once everything has been set
correctly, the Start Restore button is operated.

The Backup and Restore programs are not difficult
to use, and are certainly more user friendly than the
equivalent functions in some previous versions of
Windows. However, except where some very simple

backup and restore operation is required, it is probably best to use the wizards. These should ensure that you do not overlook anything, and that backup files can always be successfully restored. The Automated System Restore facility is an invaluable facility, and one that it is well worth using. In the past it has been slow, difficult, and expensive to implement this type of backup system. With this facility and an inexpensive hard disc added to the PC, the entire system can be backed up quite rapidly and restored again with ease.

Alternatives

Ideally a backup should be made onto CDR or CDRW discs, but this needs a third-party backup program. CDRW discs have the advantage that they can be reused, but they are more expensive than CDR discs. Another point to bear in mind is that an ordinary CDR can be read using any form of CD-ROM drive without the need for any special drivers. The same is not true for CDRW discs. Most other forms of high capacity disc also need special driver software in order to get the disc drive functioning properly.

This is no problem when you have a fully working computer that is running Windows, but it might be problematic if you have a computer that will not boot into Windows. You need to do some careful checking before using any form of backup that relies on anything other than a standard form of disc for storage. There is no point in carefully producing sets

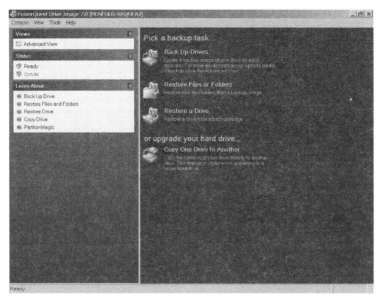

Fig.7.26 The initial screen of Drive Image

of backup discs if the image they contain can never be restored to the PC. If in doubt, stick to standard disc types, which really means a hard drive or CDRs.

Power Quest's Drive Image 7 is used in this example of producing a backup to CDRs and restoring it. There are other backup programs that no doubt work very well, and I am using Drive Image 7 here simply because it is the one installed on my PC. When this program is run under Windows XP it is possible to produce a backup from within Windows. With other backup programs and other versions of Windows it is often necessary to exit Windows and reboot into a MS/DOS or a similar operating system. This ensures that Windows does not restrict access to any files on the

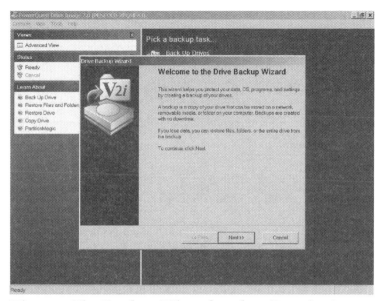

Fig.7.27 The Backup Wizard makes it easier to produce the backup

disc, but is obviously not very convenient. However, with most modern backup programs the reboot into a basic operating system is taken care of by the program, and the process may well be completely automatic.

Launching Drive Image 7 produces the initial screen of Figure 7.26, and the Backup Drives option is selected in order to start the backup process. Making the backup is made easier by the use of a wizard (Figure 7.27). Operating the Next button moves things on to the window of Figure 7.28 where the drive to be backed up is selected. Actually, in a multi-drive system it is possible to select more than one drive if desired. In this example only the boot drive (drive C)

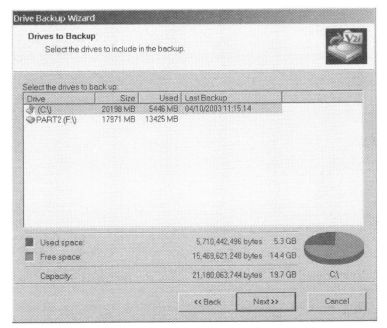

Fig.7.28 First select the drive to be backed up

will be backed up, because the other hard drive is itself a backup drive.

The destination for the backup is selected at the next window (Figure 7.29). The Local File option is used when the backup will be onto another hard disc drive. Obviously the Network option is used where the PC is on a local area network (LAN) and the backup will be placed elsewhere on the network. In this case the backup will be made to a CDRW drive, so it is the third option that is selected. The required drive can be selected using the usual file browser if the Browse button is operated.

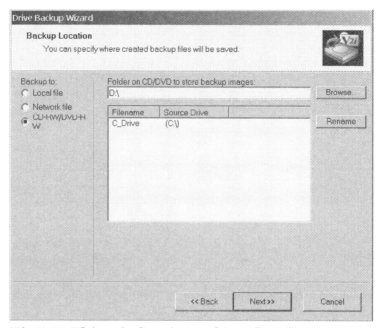

*Fig.7.29 This window is used to select the
destination drive*

The required type of compression is selected at the
next window (Figure 7.30). Data compression enables
more data to be placed on each disc in the backup
set. When making a backup to CDR or CDRW discs
the compression has the beneficial effect of reducing
the number of discs required. With a relatively slow
backup device it can also reduce the time take to
create and restore a backup. Some types of data
compress more readily than others. Some files on
the disc may already be in compressed form and will
not be amenable to further compression. On the other
hand, things like program and simple text files will

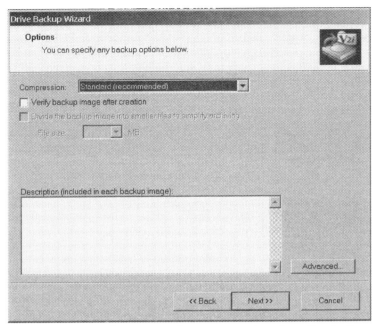

Fig.7.30 Next the type of compression is selected

often compress by a factor of three or more. In practice compression roughly halves the number of discs required. Opt for the Standard method of compression. If required, a description can be added in the textbox in the bottom section of the window (e.g. "Full backup of drive C").

The next window (Figure 7.31) simply provides a summary of the options that have been selected. If necessary, use the Back button in order to return to an earlier window so that a correction can be made. Then use the Next button to return to this window. When the right options have been selected, operate

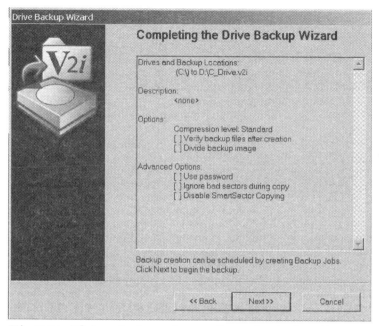

Fig.7.31 This window shows the selected options

the Next button to start making the backup. Eventually a message like the one in Figure 7.32 will appear, and the first disc is then placed in the CDR drive and the backup process starts.

A full backup is likely to require about six to twelve discs, and could obviously require substantially more than this if a large and almost full disc is being backed up. The program will prompt you each time a change of disc is required. Carefully number each disc because they must be used in the correct order when the backup is used to restore the contents of the hard disc drive. Eventually the program will indicate that

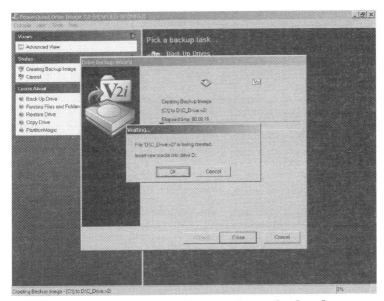

Fig.7.32 Insert the first disc and get the backup under way

the backup has been completed, and you are then returned to the main screen of Drive Image 7.

Restoring

There are facilities in the main Drive Image program for restoring data, but this route is not usable in the current context. Instead, the computer is booted using either a set of boot discs made using the program or via the Drive Image installation CD. These days practically any PC can be booted from a suitable CD-ROM, and it is probably best to use this method where the option is available. Note that this option is not available with earlier versions of Drive Image and with some other backup programs. With

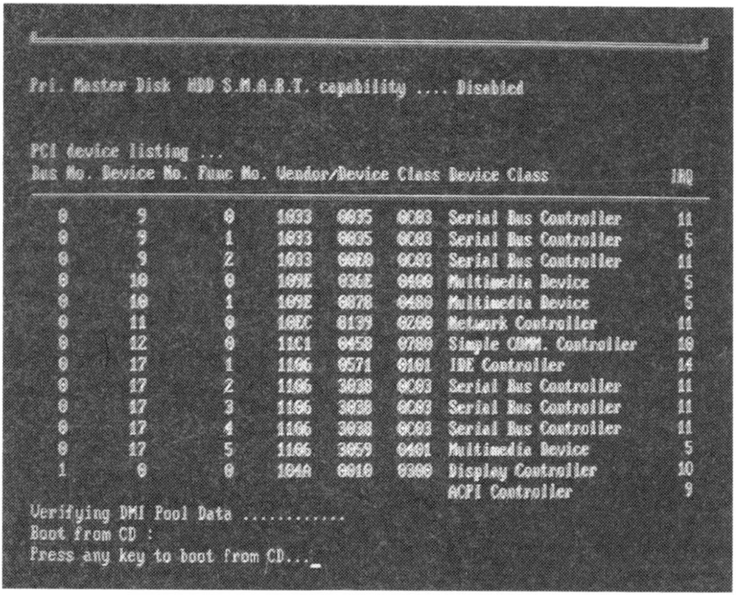

Fig.7.33 Press F2 if this message appears

some PCs it might be necessary to alter the BIOS
settings in order to boot from a CD-ROM. The
computer's operating manual should explain how to
do this. Using a set of bootable floppy discs is one
way around the problem if you do not feel confident
about dealing with the BIOS Setup program.

The computer will usually start booting from the CD-
ROM or bootable floppy disc without any preamble.
Depending on the BIOS used in your PC, it might
instead try to boot into the damaged operating system
on the hard disc unless you press a key at the right
time. If a message like the one in Figure 7.33 appears
at the bottom of the screen, immediately press F2 or

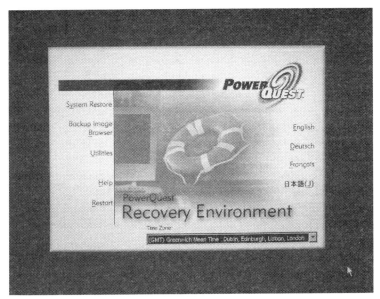

Fig.7.34 The options available from the program

whatever key the message indicates. The PC should then boot into the operating system contained on the bootable CD-ROM or floppy disc.

This will usually be MS-DOS or something similar, but the Restore program usually includes a simple Windows style user interface. Some messages will probably appear on the screen giving a brief explanation of what the program is doing. When using the floppy disc method there will usually be a boot disc and one or more program discs. Change discs when prompted. The boot process can be quite long, because the Restore program will probably scan the PC's hardware so that it can operate with the mouse, etc., you are using. Where appropriate, networking

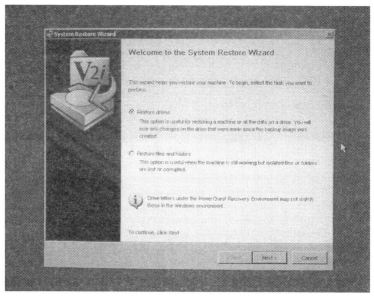

Fig.7.35 A full or partial restoration can be chosen

might be activated so that the hard disc can be restored from an image file stored on another PC on the network.

Eventually the boot and loading processes should come to an end and a screen like the one of Figure 7.34 will then be obtained. A number of options are available, but it is the System Restore facility that is needed in this case. Selecting this option moves things on to the screen of Figure 7.35 where the radio buttons provide two options. One is used to restore only certain files or folders, and the other is used to restore a complete drive. It is obviously the latter that is required here. The next screen (Figure 7.36)

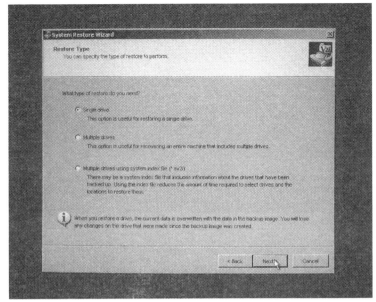

Fig.7.36 One or multiple drives can be restored

provides the option of restoring one drive or multiple drives. In this example it is only drive C that is being restored, so the single drive option is selected.

At the next screen the backup file is selected, and a file browser is available via the Browse button. Having pointed the program to the drive containing the first disc in the backup set, a message like the one in Figure 7.37 will appear. It is normal for programs that use multi-disc sets to require the first and last discs in the set before proceeding. After the program has read from the last disc you will be prompted to replace the first disc in the drive. You should then have something like Figure 7.38, with the

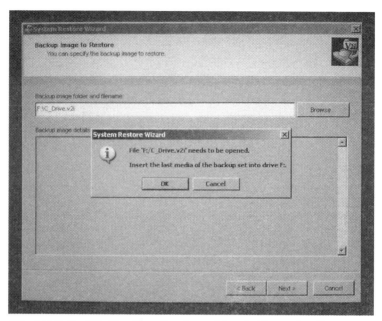

Fig.7.37 Initially the first and last discs in the set are required

screen showing the location of the backup file and some basic information for it.

Figure 7.39 shows the next screen, and here you must select the drive to be restored. Restoring the image to the wrong drive or partition will erase all the data it contains, so you must be careful to choose the right disc if there is more than one hard drive or partition. It is then just a matter of following the onscreen prompts, and changing discs when necessary. The discs in the backup set must be numbered so that you can provide them in the correct order. The program will detect the error if you should get the discs

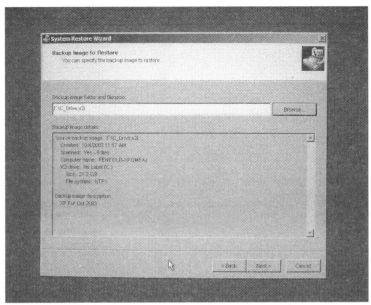

*Fig.7.38   This screen shows the backup's
            location, etc.*

muddled up, and it will not proceed until the right disc
has been placed in the drive.

Once the restoration has been completed, remove the
boot CD-ROM or floppy disc from the drive and reset
the computer. It should then boot into the newly
restored operating system. The PC should then
operate exactly as it did at the time the backup was
made. There can be minor problems such as stored
passwords being lost, and automatic login facilities
failing to work in consequence. This is due to the
password being concealed on the disc in a hidden file
that the backup program misses. You have to login
manually and then reinstate the automatic facility. Of

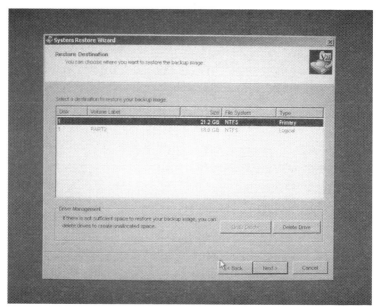

Fig.7.39 Be careful when selecting which drive to restore

course, any data or programs added since the backup was made must be reinstated in order to bring the installation fully up to date.

Points to remember

Apart from providing an easy way back to an efficient system, backing up data and system information to another drive guards against a serious attack from a virus, a hard disc failure, or other major catastrophe. Backing up system information to the main hard drive is only sufficient to guard against problems with the operating system.

Floppy discs are inadequate to cope with the large amounts of data produced by many modern applications. A CD writer, Zip drive, additional hard disc, or some other form of mass storage device is required. A mass storage device is also required in order to make a full backup of the main hard disc drive. Note that some backup programs (including the Windows XP Backup program) are not compatible with CD writers.

In order to get things back to a "lean" setup it is necessary to make a full backup of the hard drive before the system becomes bloated. Plenty of third-party backup software is available, but the Windows XP Backup utility is just about adequate for most purposes. Combined with an additional hard disc drive, this provides a fast and cost-effective method of providing a full system backup.

The Windows Backup program can be used to backup selected files, or a full backup of the hard disc can be provided. Regularly backing up the full contents of a hard disc is relatively time consuming, but restoring a full backup is the quickest way to get the computer into full working order again if a major problem occurs.

The Windows XP Backup program can be used without wizards, but for most purposes the wizards provide the easiest and most reliable means of handling backup and restore operations.

It is necessary to buy a backup program such as drive image in order to make a backup copy on CDR discs. This method has the advantage of placing the backup copy beyond the reach of viruses. Another advantage is that the cost is quite low provided your PC already has a CD writer (as most do). It is relatively slow though.

Index

Index

Index

Index

Notes

Notes